D1291661

COMPLETE SPEAKER'S

AND

TOASTMASTER'S LIBRARY

Origins and Firsts

COMPLETE SPEAKER'S

AND

TOASTMASTER'S LIBRARY

Origins and Firsts

by Jacob M. Braude

PRENTICE-HALL, INC.
Englewood Cliffs, N.J.

PRINTED IN THE UNITED STATES OF AMERICA

16461–X

COMPLETE SPEAKER'S

AND

TOASTMASTER'S LIBRARY

Origins and Firsts

1. Alma Mater

We go back to medieval times to find the origin of this term as applied to schools and colleges. A statue of Mary, mother of Christ, over the portals of a university in Germany was known as Alma Mater, fostering mother, and was applied to the school by its students. Later the term was adopted by all students and applied to their schools.

2. Anecdote

Originally this term was reserved for a story told in strict confidence. It is from the Greek *a* (or *an*) *ekdotos,* meaning not to be published or given out. Through misuse it has come to mean a story told to anybody and everybody . . . which probably is what happened to the story originally told "in strict confidence."

3. Antibiotics

While today's miracle drugs are used to save human lives, the term "antibiotic" originates from Greek words that mean "against life." The definition is not really paradoxical because these life-giving drugs are directed against bacteria and viruses, which also are forms of life.

4. Antimacassar

Ever wonder how the pretty little lace doily, pinned to the back of a chair or sofa, got such a strange unwieldy name? Here's the story: When your grandfather was a gay young blade he used a particularly messy hair oil, the ingredients of which came from Macassar (native Mangkasara), a district on the island of Celebes. His mother and wife used these doilies to protect the upholstery of their furniture from this mess. *Anti,* of course, is Latin for against.

5. April Fools' Day

There are several probable origins given for April Fools' Day. Some ascribe it to a memorable transaction between Romans and Sabines mentioned by Dionysius:

1

The Romans, about the time of the infancy of the city, wanting wives, and finding they could not obtain the neighboring women by their peaceable addresses, resolved to make use of a stratagem; and, accordingly, Romulus instituted certain games to be performed in the beginning of April (according to the Roman calendar) in honor of Neptune.

Hearing of these festivities all the families in the neighborhood poured into Rome to view the proceedings. With them came, as a matter of course, their marriageable daughters, and these being filled with admiration at the skill exhibited by the men, were easily persuaded into marrying the heroes, and many matches were arranged by this means.

Others, again, place the origin of the term "Fools' Day" to a relic of some old heathen Celtic festival; but that it is an exceedingly ancient custom can be proved by the records kept of April fool-making at the beginning of the eigtheenth century, and it appears to have been universal throughout Europe.

It is generally supposed to have come both to England and Germany from France, where one who is made an April Fool is called *Un Poisson d'Avril*, "an April fish." In Scotland the term used is *Gowk*, being from the Scotch word for "Cuckoo," signifying "a foolish person."

6. Arbor Day

This day, which now is observed in every state of the union and also the District of Columbia and Puerto Rico, dates back to the time when J. Sterling Morton, as a member of the state board of Nebraska, presented a resolution declaring the first formal observance of Arbor Day designating April 10, 1872 as the date. In the succeeding years the date continued to be changed from time to time and finally was fixed by the Nebraska legislature as April 22, which coincided with Morton's birthday. However, as of this time the date varies in different states.

7. Automation

This word was coined by Del S. Harder of the Ford Motor Company in 1946 as he was discussing plans for a new plant. At that time he said: "Let's have more mechanical handling between the transfer machines, more of that automatic business. Give us some more of that . . . that . . . automation."

2

8. Automobile Tire

An automobile tire is so named because in the early days is was considered "attire" or covering for a wheel.

9. Ballad

The word ballad comes from a word meaning "to dance" and it is thought by some that ballads were chanted while people danced. Ballads were passed on by singers and today make up some of our most interesting poetry in literature. Ballads usually tell a simple story of love and banditry.

10. Banking

Some three hundred years ago, when a man put money in an English bank, his deposit was recorded by notching a stick. The stick was then split, the bank keeping one half, the depositor the other half. Before the money could be withdrawn, the two pieces had to be matched. The depositor's half was called "bank stock," whereas the part kept by the bank was the "check."

11. Bankrupt

The origin of the word bankrupt is traced back to ancient times. An Hebraic custom required the deposit in the temple of certain sums of money in Hebraic currency. As Roman coins frequently were used, money-changers set up their tables or benches (banks) on which they kept Hebraic coins to be bought in Roman money. Money also was lent, and sometimes the changer found himself owing more than he owned. To prevent further calamity his creditors drove him from his business and broke his bench to pieces. He was then "bench-broken" or bankrupt.

12. Barber's Pole

In former times barbers served the public in the capacity of surgeons, and performed the act of bleeding, that being a favorite remedy with our ancestors. The pole represented the staff held by the person being bled, and the spiral stripes painted around it were typical of the two bandages used for twisting around the arm previous to the bleeding and after the operation had been performed. The blue stripes and stars sometimes seen probably were introduced by some barber endowed with more patriotism than love of ancient customs.

13. Basketball

The first game was played by members of the YMCA Training College at Springfield, Massachusetts, on January 20, 1892, a few days after their coach, Dr. James A. Naismith, invented the rules. The game was mainly a scheme to sop up athletic energies between the ending of the football and the beginning of the baseball seasons. The original goals were peach baskets. Players climbed a ladder to retrieve the ball. Pro basketball was played in 1898. The center jump after each goal was eliminated a quarter-century ago to cut down the advantage of seven-footers.

14. Bazooka

The rocket-projectile gun was so named because of its resemblance to the gaspipe musical instrument of Bob Burns, radio comedian of not too many years ago. Bob probably named his instrument Bazooka because of its resemblance to a bassoon, coupled with the fact that "kazoo" (sometimes called bazoo) is a toy instrument of the early 1890's.

15. Bedlam

In 1247, in England, a hospital was started, called St. Mary of Bethlehem. Two centuries later it became a hospital for the insane. Instead of being a place of quiet and healing, it became a place of disorder, confusion and discordant noises. Throughout the years the name *Bethlehem*, whenever spoken of this place, was contracted and changed into first *Bethlem* and then *Bedlam*. Now, when we think of noise and confusion, we sometimes say "The place was a bedlam."

16. Begonia Plant

The begonia owes its name to a French amateur botanist, Michel Begon, an administrator in the West Indies at the time of Louis XIV, says the National Geographic Society. The plant reached England in

1777; its culture in Belgium began in the middle of the nineteenth century. Today the begonia is to Belgium what the tulip is to the Netherlands. The bulk of Belgium's huge crop of begonia tubers is exported, mostly to the United States.

17. Big Ben

This is not the name of the clock at Westminster, but the bell which chimes the hour. It was named after Sir Benjamin Hall, who was First Commissioner of Works at the time it was cast. Incidentally, the first stroke of Big Ben, and not the last, is the exact hour.

18. Biscuit

Biscuits originated in 1550 when King Henry II of France stopped at a village baker's shop while on a tour of the provinces and ordered the baker to produce a completely new kind of cake. To seek inspiration, the desperate baker adjourned to a tavern, leaving one of his dough mixtures behind him. Anxious to save the dough from spoiling, his son rolled it into small round cakes and put them in the oven. After a while he took them out, glazed them, then put them back. When his father returned, the son produced the twice-baked (*bis cuit* in French) cakes. The king liked them.

19. Bistro

When Napoleon's regime fell in 1815, Paris was occupied by Russian soldiers. They were tired and hungry as they wandered the streets. Whenever a group of them entered a small eating place, they shouted "Bistro, bistro." In Russian that meant "Quick, quick." The Paris bistro of today, a friendly, unpretentious, and usually inexpensive eating place, evolved from the eagerness of Russian soldiers to be served after the downfall of Napoleon.

20. Blackball

When a man incurred the displeasure or wrath of the community, in ancient Athens, citizens were called upon to vote whether or not he was to be exiled. Voters were given a white ball and a black ball. One of these was to be dropped secretly into a jar, the black ball indicating exile. Paper ballots have long since replaced white and black balls but the expression remains with us.

21. Blimp

This word had its origin in the first World War in Great Britain. When the British were experimenting with lighter-than-air craft, it was found that their first model, called the "A-limp," was not satisfactory. The second type, which did function satisfactorily, was named the "B-limp." Thus the non-rigid aircraft inevitably became "the blimp."

22. Bloodhound

The bloodhound did not derive its name from the blood-thirsty nature that is implied by the animal's ability to track down fugitives. It was the first breed of dog to have a pedigree and the term "bloodhound" was used originally simply to indicate that the animal was pure-bred, or had come from "blood" or "blooded" stock.

23. Bonfire

When wars and pestilence ravaged England during the Middle Ages, fires for the burning of corpses were daily necessities. They were called fires of bone or "bonefires." When the custom of burning heretics at the stake became common, the same term was applied to pyres of these unfortunate victims. Later, open-air fires were given the same name, but by this time a less gruesome spelling was adopted.

24. Bowling

The exact origin of bowling seems to be obscure. In Germany, and in the monasteries there, to relieve the boredom of their cloistered lives, German monks set up rows of kegels—or clubs—and rolled big, rounded stones at the clubs to knock them over. Soon, German laymen discovered the pastime and by the fourteenth century bowling in alleys had become a universal sport in Germany.

Except for archery, bowling is England's oldest sport. It was declared illegal by Edward III way back in 1361, because he feared it would supplant the bow and arrow—then the principal means of defense—as a pastime. When the ban was lifted it became so popular in the fourteenth and fifteenth centuries that many noblemen had their own greens laid down.

One suggested origin of bowls is that an ancient king of Scotland amused himself by rolling the heads of his enemies along a flat meadow toward a peg stuck in the turf. There may be something in it, for even today the woods clustered around the jack are referred to as the "head."

25. Boycott

In Ireland, during the 1880's, there was a land agent for an English nobleman by the name of Captain Boycott. He must have been a pretty mean character. His harsh methods of collecting rents, and immediate eviction of those unable to pay, soon resulted in the hatred and enmity of all tenants. Thereupon the tenants and their friends devised a method of ostracism to meet the conditions. Servants and laborers refused to work for Captain Boycott; shopkeepers avoided selling him; blacksmiths would not shoe his horses; and passers-by on the street wouldn't even nod to him. Shunned by everybody, his life became unbearable, and he was forced to leave the country, a ruined and embittered man. With a deeper and more personal connotation than "ostracize" or "excommunication," boycott was immediately accepted into the English language as a needed word and newspapers soon were printing it without a capital letter. That is the way it is printed today.

26. Brass Hat

An officer is known to soldiers as a "Brass Hat." This expression goes back to the South African war of 1899–02. English officers in that war wore hats which were ornamented on the brim with gold oak leaves— which the soldiers called "brass."

27. Brass Tacks

Dry-goods stores of a generation ago were equipped with brass tacks, driven into the counters at specific distances for accurately measuring cloth. Sometimes a salesman would measure a yard of cloth by stretching it from fingertip to shoulder, but a prudent customer might suggest he "get down to brass tacks." The tacks long since have disappeared as measuring devices, but the familiar phrase has remained in our language.

28. Bribe

This word once meant "an honest scrap of bread," and its late Latin form was *briba*. The French borrowed it and used it in the sense of "a lump of bread" or "leavings of meals," or something that might be given to beggars. But its meaning degenerated morally while acquiring greater importance financially. When it first came into English it meant "a gift begged;" subsequently, "a present." In modern use the "present" frequently is a large amount of money and its purpose is to corrupt a person in a position of trust.

29. Bridge

As a game of cards for four players competing as two partnerships, bridge is one of a series of games which grew out of whist. The origin of whist is obscure, but it thrived about 150 years, beginning around 1750. Some forms of bridge supposedly existed in Constantinople and Egypt about 1865 and by 1900 had reached Paris. In England the game was first known as bridge whist and the *London Times* of January 16, 1903, referred to it as the "new game of auction bridge." Contract bridge was introduced to the United States around 1927 and today enjoys the widest popularity of any card game in history.

30. Bugle

The first bugle was made from a bull's horn, and from this it gets its name. Bugle is derived from *buculus,* "a young bull."

31. Bullfights

The ancient Greeks were really the originators of the national sport of Spain and Mexico. Their method was to turn loose a number of bulls and a like number of men in an arena and let each choose an antagonist. The best bull or man won. Julius Caesar brought the sport to Rome from where it spread to Spain, Mexico, and other countries, but in the modified form which we know today.

32. Caddie

Women have been playing golf a great deal longer than most men realize. Though golf originated as a man's game, it was played by Mary Queen of Scots as long ago as the sixteenth century. In France, she called the boys who fetched her golf balls, "cadets," pronounced "cadday;" hence "caddie."

33. Caesarean Operation

This term has no relation to the birth of Julius Caesar. It goes far back into antiquity, and the operation is supposed to have been performed by the early Greeks. The word "Caesarean" derives from the Latin past participle *caesus,* from *caedere,* meaning "to cut."

34. Candymaking

Candymaking goes back long before the twentieth century. The sweet tooth, apparently, has been catered to for at least 3,500 years. Egyptian hieroglyphics show that in 1566 B.C. confections of honey, flour, almonds and figs, were being sold in market places. In 1911 the candy bar was introduced for the first time in major league ball parks. Spectators of the national pastime spent much of their time unwrapping chocolate-coated marshmallows and peanuts.

35. Canteen

A canteen is really a cellar and is derived from the Italian *cantina,* "a wine cellar." In later years it came to be attached to a refreshment house in army barracks, and still later, to a vessel in which water or wine was carried by soldiers when on the march. Nowadays we hear a lot about canteens as places for dining or places of recreation in army encampments.

36. Cap and Gown

The general use of caps and hats in Europe came in the year 1449, when Charles VII of France entered Rouen. When the cap was of velvet, it was called *mortier;* when it was wool, it was called *bonnet.* None but kings, princes and knights were allowed to use the mortier. The cap, which was round, was used as a headdress by the clergy and graduates. When the people began wearing the cap, the students changed the round cap to a square one, and it became a symbol that they had acquired full liberty and were no longer subject to the rod of their superiors.

37. Cardinal's Red Hat

In the year 1245, at the Council of Lyons, the subjects of the newly deposed Emperor, Frederick II, were absolved by the Pope from all further allegiance to their former ruler. At the same Council, the red hat was granted to the cardinals by Pope Innocent IV, as a token that they should be ready to shed blood for the Church, and especially in a crusade, if necessary, against the deposed Emperor. It is thought that in selecting the color red, the Pope may have had in mind the words "The shield of his mighty men is made red, the valiant men are in scarlet."

38. Carpetbaggers

This was a term of scorn applied by Southern people after the Civil War to Northern business opportunists who swept over the South to exploit its prostrate condition through economic and political chicanery. They often carried carpet satchels.

39. Cartoon

These humorous drawings were first made in France and drawn on pasteboard. Pasteboard in French is *cartone*. This, in English, became cartoon.

40. Chairman

The word chairman or the phrase "taking the chair" comes from the furnishings or customs of the time when the master of the house and his lady were the only ones who owned or occupied chairs. The rest of the household, although it shared a community dining table, sat on stools or at a lower level. A guest of consequence was honored by being invited to "take the chair."

41. Chicago

The name of this large Midwestern city in northeastern Illinois has been spelled in many different ways since it was first settled. But it would seem that all forms of spelling go back to an Indian word, *shegahg*, meaning "skunk," but whose uses were synonymous with strong, pungent, mighty. The word was applied to the wild onion, to a line of Indian chiefs, to thunder, and to certain rivers among which one runs through the present city of Chicago, and bears the city's name.

42. Chinaman's Chance

This expression in sports argot has nothing to do with the inscrutable Asiatic. It dates from the 1820s, when a writer in the *Weekly Dispatch* of London referred to the light-hitting Tom Spring, whom he thought likely to break in a long fight, as "a china man," meaning a porcelain man.

43. Chinaware

Dishes and cups are called chinaware because they are made of porcelain and porcelain was first made in China and then exported. As they arrived in other countries, they gradually acquired the name chinaware to designate the fact that they came from China and were especially fine in quality and workmanship. Currently, very little chinaware is made in China but the name remains.

44. Chiseler

This name for one who cuts corners or uses unethical practices comes from the old Roman word *cisellus*, which was a metal cutting tool. Dishonest artisans used the tool to counterfeit coins, hence its derogatory meaning.

45. Christian Era

The Christian era was calculated by the monk Dionysius Exiguus in the sixth century after Christ. Dionysius, who placed Christ's birth on December 25, in the 753rd year of Rome, decided that the Roman year 754 should be the first year of the Christian era. This is 1 A.D.

46. Christmas

There are several apparent sources for the word Christmas. To the early Christians, birthdays were a pagan custom. It was unthinkable to celebrate one's own birthday, much less the birthday of Christ. It was a sacrilege even to suggest that a Divine Being had a birthday. In the next 300 years this attitude began to change, and in 354 A.D. the Bishop of Rome declared December 25 to be the anniversary of the birth of Christ.

It is also suggested the word derived from the Greco-Latin words *christos*, meaning "anointed," and *mass*, meaning "to send." These two words taken together developed into the Old English *Cristes Maesse*, or "Christ's Mass," denoting the Incarnation. This derivative has been found to be used as early as 1038.

Cristes Maesse, or "Christ's Mass," was so named because about this time the Catholic Church began to ascribe feasts to the various saints. Each saint had his own particular mass. Since the feast of the Incarnation was the greatest of all feasts, the mass on this day was called Christ's Mass.

The abbreviation Xmas had its origin in the fact that the Greek letter *chi* was written as an "X."

47. Christmas Cards

In 1843, Henry Cole of London dreamed up the idea of sending a Christmas greeting card to his friends, and originated the first Christmas card. It was a three-panel card showing a family party in the center. The side panels depicted the old tradition of feeding and clothing the needy. The wording, "A Merry Christmas and a Happy New Year," has never been surpassed. The idea caught on and by 1860 several greeting card firms had sprung up in England. In the middle 1870's, Louis Prang of Boston entered the field with religious cards.

48. Christmas Carols

The origin of carols was in Italy in the thirteenth century. The idea became popular and was taken up in France, Spain, Germany, England and other countries. Early carols were folk songs and legendary lore;

the sacred or hymnal type carol did not develop fully until the eighteenth century.

49. Christmas Crèche

The Christmas crèche, or crib, in its present form and its use outside of churches, is credited to St. Francis of Assisi. He made the Christmas crib popular through his famous celebration at Greccio, Italy, on Christmas eve, 1223, with a Bethlehem scene including five animals. It is variously reported that on this occasion Francis, then a humble priest, changed the village church into a manger, filling the chancel with hay and pulling the oxen and an ass down the aisle. Then he persuaded a young mother to sit beside them with her baby. It is reported that the clergy considered it crazy but people regarded him as a saint.

50. Christmas Seal

The seal we use now to fight tuberculosis had its origin with Einar Holboell, a Danish postmaster, in 1903. He had the idea of issuing seals to support some worthy cause. In 1904 the first seals to be sold as an official project in Denmark carried the portrait of Queen Louise. The seal idea has spread around the world.

51. Christmas Tree

There are many legends as to the origin of the Christmas tree. Reports have it that it first appeared in Strassburg, Germany, in 1608, and the custom was kept along the Rhine for 208 years and then spread over all Germany.

Other reports have it that the basic idea of the Christmas tree goes back to medieval German mystery plays, most popular of which concerned the sin of Adam and Eve and their expulsion from paradise. These plays were most often performed in the open, on large squares in front of churches, or in the church itself. On such occasions a large fir tree, decorated with apples, was used to represent the Garden of Eden. When the plays were performed inside the church the tree was surrounded by lighted candles. The tree later became popular in the home when mystery plays were no longer performed.

Although the Germans are generally regarded as originators of the Christmas tree, its history can also be traced back to several pagan traditions.

52. Christmas Tree Lights

There are several ideas as to the origin of lights on Christmas trees. It is said that Martin Luther, while strolling the countryside one Christmas eve, was taken with the brilliance of the sky and the reflection of the stars on the snow-flecked evergreen trees. When Luther returned home he tried to reproduce the scene by attaching candles to a small evergreen tree.

Others say the tradition of tree lights stems from the custom of candles on the Christmas pyramid during medieval times. The pyramid was made of graduated wooden shelves and represented Christ as the Light of the World. The candles and decorations used on the pyramid were later transferred to the tree; thus evolved the electrically-lighted Christmas tree of today.

53. Cigar Bands

When cigars first appeared on the market about 1800, bands of plain paper were used by the ladies of Spain to keep their fingers from being stained by the tobacco. From this it was but a short step to the highly colorful gold and embossed bands used today for the purpose of brand identification or advertising.

54. Cigarette

The cigarette is said to have originated with artillerymen in 1799 at the Siege of Acre. A big pipe which had supplied the men with tobacco was destroyed by a shot fired in battle. Famished for a smoke, one of the men conceived the idea of rolling some tobacco in paper which had been used for making gunpowder spills. The men took a liking to the cigarette that was thus formed and continued using it even after the siege. The first cigarette factory of any importance was established in 1850 in St. Petersburg, Russia, now Leningrad.

55. Cocktail

It is said that this word was born during the American Revolution when a barmaid who served Colonial and allied French officers their evening drinks decided on an extra touch. She garnished them (the drinks, not the officers) with tail feathers of chickens stolen from a British sympathizer. This so delighted one of the Frenchmen that he shouted bilingually "Vive le coq's tail." The name stuck, and now denotes any drink into which fruit, flavoring, feathers or some other alien item is mixed.

56. Cocktail Hour

One afternoon in the 1800's, a man entered the establishment of a New Orleans druggist named Antoine Amedee Peychaud. Peychaud decided that the best prescription for the man, who wasn't well, would be a shot of brandy and bitters. Having nothing handy to serve it in, he used an egg cup in which he usually mixed other prescriptions.

An egg cup of the type Peychaud used is called a *coquetier* and pronounced "kok-tyay" in French-speaking New Orleans. When the man told his friends about the good-tasting drink the druggist had served him, the demand for the drink grew. Cafes, hurrying to cash in on the new fad, advertised the Kok-tyays with window signs and featured them on their menus. Eventually, *coquetier*, or Kok-tyay, was corrupted and became cocktail. So from a simple egg cup came the pleasant ritual known today the world over—the cocktail and the cocktail hour.

57. Coffee

Long before coffee was used as a drink it was known as a medicine. In France and England it was a cure-all for everything from drunkenness to smallpox. Doctors prescribed it to purify the body. It was also used as a gargle. In Turkey, coffee was so important that in the marriage ceremony a man had to promise never to permit his wife or wives to be without coffee beans.

There are many other legends as to the origin of this beverage and according to one, coffee was discovered by a shepherd in Arabia who noticed that his flock was stimulated whenever the sheep ate coffee berries. He brewed some of the beans himself and found the product tasteful as well as stimulating. However, as a beverage, coffee did not really develop until someone decided to roast the coffee bean.

58. Coffee Break

The coffee break didn't become a recognized part of the business scene until the early 1940's, but it has been going on a long time. The practice spread from Arabia, where coffee was discovered, westward through Turkey and thence to Europe and the British Isles.

In eighteenth century England, merchants transacted much of their business in coffee houses, and the same was true in Colonial America. Lloyd's of London had its beginnings in a coffee house. The first home of the New York Stock Exchange was one of these redolent rendezvous, the Tontine Coffee House, which was located on lower Wall Street.

The coming of World War II and its attendant pressures revived the custom of pausing for rest and mild stimulation over a cup of the popular beverage. The coffee break has become so common that today between 74 and 94 percent of workers in the United States and Canada recess daily for intervals of five to fifteen minutes or more around the coffee urn.

59. Cop

Generally believed to be an abbreviation of *copper,* slang for police officer. But it could derive from the verb cop, meaning "to capture." Legal Latin for a writ is *capias,* "you may seize."

Another source says that in early Colonial days, night watchmen wore large copper badges for purposes of identification. There was no missing these badges, so the nickname "copper" followed as a matter of course. Later, in accordance with custom, it was shortened to cop.

60. Cotton Gin

Eli Whitney, while struggling to find an easier way to get the seeds out of cotton bolls than by hand-picking, looked out a window and saw a fox trying to get his dinner out of a chicken coop in the yard. The fox clawed at the wire, and while he got no chicken, succeeded in pulling out plenty of feathers. This experience gave Whitney the beginning of the answer to his problem—a claw or rake that would pull the cotton fibres through a grid and leave the seeds behind.

61. Cow College

The term cow college gots its start in 1890 when the first collegiate dairying course began at the University of Wisconsin.

62. Crow's Nest

The ancient Vikings actually carried crows on the little platform on the masts of their ships. When lost they would release one of the birds and follow it as it flew towards the nearest land. Hence, the name for this little platform in these days of compasses, radio and radar.

63. Curfew

Literally, "cover the fire," from the French *couvre le feu*. The peasants of France, during the Middle Ages, were required to cover or extinguish their fires at night, a bell being rung to notify them of the exact time this was to be done. The Normans, when conquering England, extended the meaning of the bell as a signal for all citizens to leave the streets and public places and return to their homes.

64. Dark Horse

This term, now used in politics for a candidate brought forth at the last moment, had its beginning on the race track. It seems that a Sam Flynn of Tennessee had a coal black horse named Dusky Pete. Short of funds, or means of transportation, Flynn actually rode his horse from town to town, track to track. While Dusky Pete was sluggish when coming into town, he invariably snapped out of his apparent stupor on the track and won a great many races.

65. Decimal Coinage

Our decimal coinage was devised by Thomas Jefferson. Two years before Gouverneur Morris, a clerk in the office of his uncle, Robert Morris, had conceived the idea of applying the decimal system to the notation of money. The details of the system devised by Morris were so cumbrous and awkward as almost to neutralize the simplicity of the leading idea. Jefferson rescued the fine original conception by proposing our present system of dollars and cents, which was adopted by Congress in 1785.

66. Dewey Decimal System

This method of classification of books uses the numbers 000 to 999 to cover general fields of knowledge and narrows the system to fit special subjects by the use of decimal points. It was developed by Melvil Dewey, who originated the system while librarian at Amherst College. The system, adopted by most libraries in the United States and in many foreign countries is described in Dewey's book, *A Classification and Subject Index for Cataloguing and Arranging the Books and Pamphlets of a Library.*

67. Dixie

Here too, the origin of this affectionate nickname for the southern part of the United States is confused and lost in varied legend. There are those who think it stems from the Mason-Dixon line, which was originally established in 1763 to settle a dispute between the lord proprietors Baltimore and Penn. The names of the surveyors, Charles Mason and Jeremiah Dixon, were applied to the line which was marked by milestones. This line later marked the boundaries of the free and slave states.

Another version of its historical origin is that years ago a bank in New Orleans issued notes in both French and English because there were so many people in that city who could read only French. On the French ten-dollar note was printed the word *dix*, which means "ten." It was most popular of these notes and in time was called a "dixie." The bank became known as the bank of the "dixies," and little by little the South was nicknamed the "land of the dixies."

And still another tells us that a kindly slave owner named Dixie, in New York, sold his slaves to a Southern cotton planter, when slavery was forbidden in the North. His former slaves talked so much of "Dixie's land," where they had been happy, that it came to be regarded as a sort of paradise. When D. D. Emmett wrote the song *Dixie* he may not have known that "Dixie's land" was in the North, or he may have thought the song would have more appeal if it were placed "way down south in de land ob cotton." At any rate, nowadays when we speak of Dixie we are referring to the South.

68. Doubleheader

Baseball appropriated this term for "two games played in a single afternoon" from railroading, where it means "two engines pulling a single train."

69. Doughnut

One legend credits the invention of the American style doughnut, with a hole, to a Maine sea captain named Hansen Gregory. Sailors on his ship, who wanted to steer and eat at the same time, could slip a doughnut over the spokes of the ship's wheel.

70. Eavesdrop

Early English cottages were provided with over-hanging thatched roofs to prevent rainwater running down the walls. The spot on the ground where the eaves dripped was called, naturally, eavesdrip. Between the eavesdrip and the wall of the structure was a convenient place for persons of curious intent to stand and overhear what the occupants were saying. Such persons were known as eavesdroppers. And they still are, although eavesdrips have long since been replaced with gutters and downspouts.

71. Etiquette

The original meaning of the word etiquette is "ticket" or "label." The French royal court was once noted for its elaborate functions and for the strict rules of behavior at them. Tickets were given to persons invited to the court, and on the backs of the tickets were outlined the formalities expected of guests. *Etiquette*, the name of the ticket, eventually was applied to the rules of court behavior. The word entered the English language in the seventeenth century and was broadened in meaning—the rules of proper behavior anywhere in society.

72. Father's Day

It was in the spring of 1919 that Mrs. John Bruce Dodd of Spokane, Washington, got the idea for Father's Day—an idea that came during a Mother's Day sermon that was full of adulation for motherhood. The preacher was eloquent though he didn't even mention the word "father." Mrs. Dodd's mother had died when she was but a mere child and her thoughts naturally turned to her father who was left with the responsibility of rearing six children. She thought it would be nice to honor him and others like him and took her plan to the preacher who drafted a resolution and on June 10, 1919, the first Father's Day was observed in Spokane. The first observance of truly national proportions was in 1922 on the third Sunday of June.

73. Fee

This common term for "fixed charge" for professional services—as in law, medicine, and art—is one of our earliest words. It originally meant "cattle," the primitive essential to community life, and the earliest instrument of barter . . . hence money. Anglo-Saxon *feoh* means both "cattle" and "money." Feud, foe, and fiend also fit in here somewhere but the trail is faint and complex.

74. Fiasco

This rather common word which means "failure" comes from the Italian name for common bottle. It was the practice of ancient Venetian glass blowers, when noticing the slightest flaw in the article upon which they were working, to discard it for later conversion into a common bottle. What might have been a beautiful Venetian vase was now a fiasco. In this manner failure and fiasco became associated. From fiasco we also get flask and flagon, other forms of containers.

75. Fifth Column

This term came into popular usage during World War II and was applied to spies operating in enemy country, acquiring information, obstructing military preparations, alarming, confusing and dividing the populace. However, it was first used during the Spanish Civil war (1936–39) by General Mola who announced that he had four columns of soldiers advancing on Madrid and a fifth column of sympathizers within the city that would attack the defenders from the rear. In Paris, during its occupation by the Germans, it is said that editors always published the pictures of traitors, or citizens fraternizing with the enemy, in the fifth column of their newspapers . . . a none-too-subtle inference as to their loyalty.

76. Filibuster

The word is derived from *filibusteros.* Originally, the term was applied to those who for power, loot, or adventure organized expeditions in the United States for the invasion of Latin-American countries. These were primarily West Indian pirates who scourged the southern seas in small craft called "filibotes." Hence, use of the term for tactics by minorities that oppose majorities. Currently, filibustering has come to mean a parliamentary device to delay or prevent action by the majority. Its philosophical foundation results in the protection of minority rights. Senate historians say American filibusters of a sort even occurred in Congress as far back as 1789.

77. Flag Day

This occasion as we know it, was originated by Dr. Bernard J. Cigrand who made a practice of flying the national flag over the school where he taught near Fredonia, Wisconsin, every June 14th. In 1916, President Wilson officially made June 14th Flag Day, and that custom still prevails.

There are other historians who contend that it was a Professor George Bolch, a principal of a free kindergarten for the poor in New York City, who arranged for observance of Flag Day on June 14, 1889. This event attracted great attention, so much so that the New York State Department of Education decided it should be observed in all public schools and the New York legislature enacted a law soon thereafter ordering the state superintendent of public schools to prepare a program making special provision for observance of Flag Day and putting it on the same level as Lincoln's Birthday, Washington's

Birthday, and Memorial Day. In 1897 the governor of the State of New York, by proclamation, required the United States flag to be displayed over all public buildings and there are some who maintain that this was the first official recognition of Flag Day in the United States by anyone other than school authorities. However, there seems to be some proof that as a result of a resolution adopted by the Pennsylvania Society of Colonial Dames, the mayor of Philadelphia ordered the flag to be flown over all public buildings. The exact date when this was done has not been definitely determined.

78. Flag, United States

Tradition has assigned the honor of having designed the first stars and stripes to Mrs. John Ross, better known as Betsy Ross, an expert needlewoman who maintained an upholstery shop at 329 Arch Street, Philadelphia. The story goes that she was approached by General Washington, Robert Morris and Colonel Ross, members of a committee appointed by Congress, who submitted a rough sketch to her recommending a five-pointed star rather than the six-pointed star of heraldry. Mrs. Ross demonstrated how a five-pointed star could be cut with one deft snip of the scissors. Her grandson, William J. Canby, first made this story known in a paper read before the Historical Society of Pennsylvania in 1870.

More recently, it has been suggested that one Francis Hopkinson, of New Jersey, was the first to have proposed a flag with stars and stripes to be the national flag for the new-born republic.

79. Four-H Clubs

The Four-H clubs originated with a rural youth movement in Macoupin County, Illinois, in 1900. Selected seed corn was distributed to 500 boys with the suggestion that they plant it and exhibit it at the County Farmers' Institute. Similar clubs were organized in 1902 in Clark County, Ohio, and by 1909 the movement had extended to twenty states. The Smith-Lever agricultural act passed by Congress in 1914 established the 4-H clubs as a national organization. The symbol of the club is the four-leaf clover and the four H's are the initials of heart, head, hands, and health.

80.   Freedom of the Press

In America freedom of the press was established in 1735. John Peter
Zenger published in his *New York Weekly Journal* a report of election
frauds and an exposure of graft and malfeasance by the Royal Governor William Cosby. Zenger was arrested for "seditious libel" and a bail
was set so high that he could not raise the money. Alexander Hamilton,
ablest colonial lawyer, defended him, admitted that Zenger printed the
charges but contended they were true. Zenger was acquitted, and the
Fourth Estate allowed its freedom.

81.   Friday the 13th

Scholars have spent many years trying to pinpoint the origin of
various superstitions, particularly that relating to Friday the 13th.

One theory links together the fact that Christ was crucified on
Friday and that there were thirteen present at the Last Supper, with
Judas counted as the thirteenth.

Another theory links these facts: in ancient England, hangings were
conducted on Fridays; there were thirteen steps to the gallows and the
hangman was paid thirteen pence.

There is some evidence that a farm expert of ancient Greece named
Heseid was superstitious about the number thirteen. In 850 B.C. he
warned against sowing seed on the "13th of the waxing month."

82.   Garrison Finish

The term "a Garrison finish" means any competition in which one of
the participants comes from behind to win. It is a racing term for "a
poor start but a good finish," and owes its origin to Edward H.
(Snapper) Garrison, one of the most famous jockeys in turf history,
whose favorite tactic in racing was to keep his horse back during the
early part of a race and then win by a sudden burst of speed in the
final stretch. The phrase became a byword in 1886 when Garrison came
from nowhere with an outsider, "Dutch Roller," to win the Great
Eastern Handicap at Sheepshead Bay. Garrison retired in 1897 and
died in New York in 1931.

83. Get in Dutch

This old saying means "to fall into disfavor, or disgrace, or some serious trouble." The expression began when Britain and Holland were battling for control of trade on the high seas. The English tried to discredit everything Dutch by propaganda methods. Thus, everything Dutch was considered bad.

84. Get One's Dander Up

Dander is a contraction of "damned anger." It was first used when folks were provoked, but not sufficiently provoked to swear about it.

85. G. I.

This nickname for the United States soldier became common during World War II. Its meaning derives from the words "Government Issue." The fact that everything a soldier wore, from socks to tunic, trousers and hat, and everything he ate, or was paid, was issued by the Government of the U.S. made him, in fact, a complete "Government Issue."

86. Gift Horse

The complete expression "Don't look a gift horse in the mouth" is based upon the practice of determining the age of a horse by examining its teeth. A mild admonition against inquiring too minutely into the intrinsic value of a gift, it is found in Latin as early as 400 A.D. and is literally reproduced in Italian, French, Spanish, and German, as well as in English.

87. Gilding the Lily

Literally, this expression means "to improve the unimprovable." It is really a misquote of the Shakespearean phrase "painting the lily."

88. Glass Manufacture

The origins of glass-making are lost in antiquity but it is known that the Egyptians used glass articles more than 4,000 years ago. Glass objects believed to have been made as far back as that have been found in ancient Mesopotamia, now part of Iraq.

Legend also has it that in the Middle East, a caravan of Phoenician merchants built a pile of stones in the desert on which to support their cooking vessels. When their meal was ready and the pots were removed, these merchants found a clear, transparent substance under the pots which, when cold, could be picked up and looked through. The stones which they used were found to be natron which consisted of an impure form of sodium carbonate and this, under the heat of the fire, combined with desert sand, formed sodium silicate which is, in fact, a form of glass. Glass as we know it, however, was not manufactured in England until the middle of the sixteenth century.

89. Gob

Although there are numerous explanations for the origin of the use of these initials in reference to the United States sailor, it seems to stem from the French *garde de l'eau,* meaning "water guard." It was then carried over into the English language as "gobby loo," which in a short while was shortened to the familiar gob.

90. Gobbledygook

This expression first came into use during World War II and is currently defined to mean "inflated, involved, and obscure verbiage characteristic of the pronouncements of officialdom." Congressman Maury Maverick of Texas is given credit for its invention. When asked how he happened to invent the word, he said: "Perhaps I was thinking of the old bearded turkey gobbler back in Texas who strutted around in ludicrous pomposity while gobbedy-gobbling. At the end of his gobbles there was a sort of gook to serve as an exclamation point."

91. God Bless You

This phrase is said to have been originated by the devout Pontiff St. Gregory the Great, who in the year 750 appointed a form of prayer to be said by persons sneezing. At that time it was believed that the air was filled with great impurities and many who sneezed violently were in danger of expelling their souls and that this danger could be counteracted by a proper prayer or phrase.

92. Golf

There are some who claim that golf is a game of Dutch origin and others who contend it was invented by a Scottish lady who objected to her husband drinking at home. The earliest mention of golf to be found in print is contained in Adamson's *Mirthful Mournings,* published in 1638.

There is evidence that golf was being played in the middle of the fifteenth century and that because of its popularity ordinances were passed restricting the playing of it. King James IV banned the game altogether, probably because it interfered with the practice of archery at that time.

93. Gone to the Devil

Near the Temple Bar on London's Fleet Street was a tavern known as the "Devil and St. Dunstan." Many lawyers at the end of court frequented it and when one left his office to visit the tavern he was likely to put up a notice to that effect on his door reading, "Gone to the Devil"—Devil being the tavern's abbreviated name. The sign became such a common sight that it finally took on the meaning of "going to ruin."

94. Good Friday

The day of Jesus' crucifixion probably originally was known as God's Friday. But whether God's or Good, it was a term that carried a happy connotation.

An opposite theory holds that the Germanic people called it *Karfreitag, kar* being a derivative of an old Gothic word, *kara,* meaning "black" or "mourning," and so *Karfreitag* meant "Black" or "Grieving Friday," which conception of Good Friday has more or less dominated the Church's observance of it down through the ages.

95. Gossip

This word originally denoted a person bound to another by religious ceremony, such as a sponsor in baptism, and came from Anglo-Saxon *godsibb—sib* meaning "related to God." Godparents were expected to form a close and intimate relationship with the family whose child they sponsored. The word has degenerated sadly in meaning and from this mood of confiding intimacy, it has taken on its present meaning of "newsmonger" or "tattle."

96. Gotham

A nursery rhyme entitled *The Merry Tales of the Mad Men of Gotham,* published in the middle of the sixteenth century, describing a legendary village in England whose inhabitants were notorious for their foolishness, seems to be the recognized source of the name Gotham, which was applied to New York by Washington Irving in 1807 in the humorous periodical, *Salmagundi,* because salmagundi was a mixed dish of chopped meat and pickled herring with oil, vinegar, pepper, and onions, and therefore a heterogeneous mixture of potpourri. The word Gotham today, as we know it, means "a village or city where they have a mixed population."

97. Go West, Young Man

Although Horace Greeley usually is credited with being the first to use this expression, it appears that John L. Soule of the *Terre Haute* (Indiana) *Express* was the first to use it some time during the year 1851. Greeley merely quoted the phrase in an editorial which he wrote for the *New York Tribune.* He readily disclaimed authorship when he published the original Soule article in its entirety.

98. Grapevine

Every business organization, every government bureau, seems to have a method of communication faster and more accurate than telegraph, telephone, radio . . . or even telepathy. It is an easy matter to compare the devious routes of rumors with the twisting turns of a grapevine, but not to track them down.

99. Grass Widow

There are three different versions of the origin of this term. According to one story, the expression dates back to the days when Britain kept an army in India, where its barracks usually were in hot coastal areas. Thus it was that during the hottest periods the British officers sent their wives and children to the cooler hill districts where there was pleasant green grass and when these officers were asked, would remark jokingly: "I've sent my wife to grass." Thus the term came to be applied to a woman temporarily deprived of her husband's company.

Another version has it that the Forty-niners put their wives "out to grass," that is, to board with some family while they were prospecting for gold.

A third attributed source is that a grass widow is really a corruption of grace widow, from the French *veuve de grace*, which means "a widow by grace or dispensation of the Pope."

So take your choice!

100. Greenhorn

This term, which is more than 300 years old and refers to an inexperienced person, was first applied to a deer or other animal with green or fresh horns.

101. Grocer

Originally a grocer was one who dealt only with gross lots or large quantities. In other words, he was a wholesaler. Retailer, on the other hand, meant one who dealt in such small items that records were kept by a tally system. At first grocers dealt in almost anything salable— fish, hawks, etc.—but as importers, they began to specialize in the more lucrative spice trade. This in turn led them gradually into foods and small kitchen wares. According to Dr. Bergen Evans, a wholesale grocer is strict redundancy, while a retail grocer is quite a contradiction.

102. Grog

This spirit, which is usually served on board British naval ships, came into the language in a roundabout way from Admiral Edward Vernon (1684–1757). His men nicknamed him Old Grog from his habit of walking the quarter-deck in all weather in a grogram cloak. It was he who introduced into the Navy the practice of serving rum mixed with water, and to this concoction the name grog was applied and it has persisted throughout the years.

103. Gunny Sack

This word has been traced to India. It is from Sanscrit, *goni*, meaning "sack" or "bag" made from the coarse fibers of jute. Thus, when we say gunny sack we are really saying sack-sack or bag-bag.

104. Gymnasium

In their games in ancient Greece, athletes were not impeded by costumes. *Gymnos* is the Greek word for "nude"; hence, the word gymnasium would seem to mean "a place where one might exercise in the nude."

105. Hades

Originally the word Hades was applied to the god of the underworld and not to the place which is known as Hell. When the revised version of the *Bible* was published in 1885, it substituted Hades for Hell in a number of instances, apparently because it seemed to be a better translation of the original Greek word.

106. Hallowe'en

As we know it today, Hallowe'en seems to have begun with the ancient pagan Druids of Great Britain, who began their year on November 1, at which time witches and hobgoblins were supposed to have had their last fling of the year. With the coming of Christianity, the "New Year's Day" became "All Saints Day," and the evening before became known as "All Hallows' Eve." It is from this mixture of superstition and religion that we get the present Hallowe'en with its costumes, etc.

Scottish children first carved jack-o'-lanterns from large turnips instead of from pumpkins. Also in Scotland, people believed that women who had sold their souls to the devil changed into witches on

Hallowe'en, and that they flew up their chimneys on broomsticks, attended by black cats.

It was the Irish who started the custom of going from door to door asking for food or money. The "trick or treat" custom employed by children today dates back to seventeenth century Ireland when peasants sought luxuries for a feast at the doors of the wealthy. However, the idea of the householder forestalling a prankish trick by coming across with a treat seems to be strictly an American custom.

107. Ham Actor

This is a synonymous term for "a poor performer, or amateur," especially in the field of sports or on the stage. There are several given origins. One tells us that actors, long before grease paint was invented, coated their faces with ham fat, which simplified removal of makeup after the performance.

An English version leans toward ascribing the origin to the cockney pronunciation of amateur, *h'amateur,* which later was abbreviated to the one-syllable word *h'am.*

108. Hammock

Sailors who accompanied Columbus to the New World found the Carib Indians using this device not only for sleeping, but as a means of transporting their children. Finding these more cool and comfortable than sleeping on the open deck, the sailors introduced that which we now call hammocks to their native Europeans upon their return. The word comes from the Spanish *hamaca,* of West Indian origin.

109. Handicap

This would appear to be a contraction of "hand-in-cap," the old English game which consisted of bartering articles, with contestants giving "boots" or odds as decreed by an umpire. The players were required to deposit forfeit money in a cap, and hand-in-cap would seem to indicate the method of drawing lots.

In the eighteenth century the term was applied to advantages allowed inferior contestants in horse racing and other sports and still later took on the meaning of "any encumbrance."

110. Handkerchief

The word kerchief came to us originally from the French *couvre-chef,* which would mean "a covering for the head." The English added "hand" and gave it the meaning "a covering for the head held in the hand." Thus when we say "pocket handkerchief" we really mean "a covering for the head which is held in the hand and contained in the pocket."

111. Handshaking

In earlier and less civilized times, a shaking of hands was a way of proving that neither "shaker" was concealing a knife or other lethal weapon, and anyone who would not shake hands willingly was regarded with grave suspicion. The original handshake was a double-hand clasp, indicating that both hands were empty. With the coming of more chivalrous times, the present-day single-handed handshake came into vogue.

112. Hat in the Ring

This phrase was originated by Theodore Roosevelt in 1912 when he became a candidate for the presidency on the Bull Moose ticket. It means "to declare entrance into contention for the nomination."

113. Haywire

A tangled and twisted mass of wire taken from bales of hay is enough to suggest the origin of the phrase "when everything goes haywire." Added to this is the fact that as a rule when anything on the farm breaks down, the farmer's first effort at mending begins with the use of haywire which frequently becomes hopelessly entangled.

114. Headline, Newspaper

United States newspapers began to use headlines for their articles when hundreds of thousands of immigrants started arriving annually from various parts of the Old World, and their first need was to learn the English language. It seems they carried their food to work wrapped

31

in newspapers and during the luncheon periods spelled out the larger words as they sat munching their bread and meat. The larger the print, the easier it was for them to learn, and so enterprising publishers started using four-inch wood block type and red ink on their front pages and from that time forward the newspaper headline has continued to function as a briefing or picture of the day's news.

115. Hello

As a telephone greeting, the word hello seems to have been originated by Thomas A. Edison. In the early days of the telephone people used to say "Are you there?" (a phrase still in use in England) or something of a similar nature. The story is told that one day Mr. Edison responded to a ring on his phone by shouting "hello" into the mouthpiece. Others were quick to pick up the practice and so the word hello has gone around the world and is used in many other countries as a form of telephone greeting.

Another version tells us that many years ago people greeted each other with the salutation "Hail to," which naturally became slurred together into "hallo" and finally ended up as "hello." The English, French, German and Dutch still have their "hallo" and the Spanish their "hola."

116. Here's Mud in Your Eye

This familiar toast, according to observation, is related both to "bottoms up" and "quickie." For example, if you *up* a glass of wine too *quick*, in your enthusiasm to honor a friend or celebrity, you may splash the dregs in your eyes or his. Dregs are equal to sediment, and sediment is equal to mud.

117. High Horse

The knight of old, clad in armor and equipped with lance and shield, required a large, strong (high) horse to support him, in contrast with the smaller horse he used for hunting. Parading through a village in all his regalia, the knight was at once a fearsome and superior being to the lowly peasant forced to travel on his own two feet. Thus the expression "get down off your high horse" in the sense of "quit acting as if you are above us." We have many similar expressions such as overbearing, up-stage, high hat—the latter gaining significance because the top hat was worn only by the so-called upper classes.

118. Highway Divider

It was a woman driver, Dr. June A. Carroll of Indio, California, who first painted a line, in 1912, along a one-mile stretch of treacherous highway to help uncertain travelers find their way. Shortly afterward the California Highway Commission adopted the idea which has become standard throughout the world.

119. Hitchhike

The exact origin of this word is unknown but it apparently stems from the days when two men had to go on a journey with only one horse between them. One would start out on horseback, the other on foot. At a predetermined point the one on horseback would dismount, hitch the horse to a convenient tree and continue on via foot. Then the man who started on foot would catch up and pass the former rider. While alternating "hitching" and "hiking" the two travelers eventually reached their destination.

Another version dates coinage of this word to coincide with the period of training of American boys in military camps in the first World War. Making their way home on a brief furlough, the young men would "hike" until a car or truck approached their way and then they would "hitch" a ride. The term soon thereafter passed into the general language and has become a recognized form of travel.

120. Hobo

This word is a corruption of "hoe boy." During the settling of the western half of the United States, farmers were in constant need of hired help. As planting weather crept from south to north, and harvesting weather crept from north to south, a group of transient workers, hoe on shoulder, drifted from farm to farm selling their labor. With the coming of farm machinery these men were thrown out of work, but continued drifting, begging for handouts. The term "hoe boy" became hobo, and soon was a synonym for tramp and vagrant.

121. Hobson's Choice

Tobias Hobson, a seventeenth century Englishman, was the first man in England to let out hackney horses. When a traveler came to his stable to hire a horse, he was required to take the one nearest the door so that each customer was equally served according to chance, and Hobson's choice came to mean "choice without alternative."

122. Hockey

There is doubt as to the exact origin of the modern game of ice hockey, some contending that its name comes from the French *hoquet*, meaning "a shepherd's crook," others leaning toward the view that it is an adaptation of field hockey, a game based upon knocking an object through a goal. Games of this sort are traceable back to the pre-Christian era. The modern game of hockey was developed in the late nineteenth century. In 1883 the Wimbledon Club of England drew up rules for the game and it has continued to be a popular sport for both men and women and is an Olympic games event for men. Ice hockey gained popularity among the students of McGill University in Montreal during the 1870's and by 1885 an amateur league had been formed in Canada. The National Hockey League was organized in 1908 with all Canadian teams. Boston, in 1924, became the first United States city to obtain a franchise.

123. Hokum

This is a happy combination of *hocus* and *bunkum* and means "a sentimental or melodramatic device for attracting attention, stimulating emotion, or winning support"—often for a questionable proposition.

124. Hoodlum

The story goes that there was once a newspaper reporter in San Francisco who, in attempting to coin a name for a gang of young ruffians, hit upon the idea of taking the leader's name and reversing it.

The leader's name was Muldoon, but the reporter wrote it as Noodlums. His handwriting was not easily decipherable and the compositor set it up in type as Hoodlums. Thus hoodlum has become the name for a street tough and has remained so ever since.

125. Hoodwink

Bergen Evans tells us that originally this word meant literally to blindfold, to cover the face so that the one covered could not see (and sometimes so that he could not be identified). Criminals were hoodwinked at their executions to spare them; witnesses were hoodwinked in dangerous trials, to protect them. It now is used solely in its metaphorical sense: to blindfold mentally, to prevent one from seeing the truth, so that he might be the more easily deceived.

126. Hoosier

The term Hoosier has been applied to Indianans since the beginning of the nineteenth century. In 1830, the term appeared in a poem which was printed in the *Indianapolis Journal*. There is no satisfactory explanation of its origin. The oldest theory claims that it comes from the phrase "who's here." Others advance the theory that it may have been derived from the word "hussar"—a member of a cavalry unit of any of several European armies, who usually wore bright uniforms. Some claim it originated from the word "husher," which means a bully who at a gathering could easily "hush" or quiet someone.

127. Horsepower

Power is the rate at which energy is being spent, or the rate at which work is being done. Though it may be expressed in terms of horsepower, it bears no exact relation to animal horsepower. What we term horsepower is so called because it originated from the results of experiments carried out with strong draft horses by James Watt more than a century ago. He wished to find out the rate at which a horse, under average conditions, does its work, and he fixed this rate, as a round figure, at 550 foot-pounds of work a second, or 33,000 foot-pounds a minute—that is to say, work equivalent to that needed to raise a weight of 550 pounds one foot high in one second. Watt took this as the value of one horsepower, although he realized that it was a higher rate of work than an average horse can maintain for a full day. Of course, a horse, if stirred by a whip, can exert a much greater effort, but only for a very short time.

128. Horseshoe

According to legend, the ancient Greeks originated the horseshoe to protect the feet of their horses. The first form of shoe was a slipper made of a kind of fiber called Spanish broom (sparta), used as a binding for the diseased feet of both horses and cattle. The Romans called this safeguard for tender feet the *solea spartea*, or "broom sandal."

The Greeks and Romans later extended the idea to a more permanent shoe for horses and mules and hammered it out of metal, such as iron. It was bound on the hoof and not fastened with nails like the modern horseshoe. Later, the *solea ferrea*, "iron shoe," had seven holes for nails. Since the shoe resembled the crescent moon, it became a good luck symbol.

129. Hot Dog

Up to the time of the St. Louis World's Fair of 1904, the vendors who sold hot sausages, which we know as wieners or franks, furnished white gloves to their customers because the tidbit was too hot to hold in bare fingers. Human nature being what it is, too many customers forgot to lay down the gloves when they finished eating. One day at the St. Louis Fair one such vendor lost all his white gloves before noon. He was lamenting his luck to a baker friend who suddenly had an idea. He went back to his bake shop and soon returned with a supply of elongated rolls baked to fit the long sausages. The "hot dog" was born, even though it did not get its name until later.

Competing vendors who sold flat beef patties quickly put them between round rolls to produce today's "hamburger." Which really came first, or which sold the most at St. Louis, it is doubtful if anyone can really say.

At any rate it was several years before the "hot dog" got its name. Vendors at the Polo Grounds in New York City called the cooked franks "dachshund sausages." During ball games and other sporting events, the hawkers' cry of "red hot dachshund sausages" inspired Tad Dorgan, the cartoonist, to sketch a talking sausage complete with feet and tail. Taking their cue from this popular cartoon, the hawkers shortened their cry to "hot dogs."

130.   Hotel Register

The modern hotel register dates from a law in France in 1407, compelling the keeper of an inn to keep a book containing the names of all lodgers.

131.   Ice Cream

The history of ice cream goes back thousands of years. It was first recorded in the first century A.D. when Nero Claudius Caesar (54–68 A.D.), then Emperor of Rome, ordered some snow brought by fast runners from nearby mountains. Fruit juices and flavorings were added to the snow.

Another version tells us that Marco Polo, famed explorer and adventurer, found recipes for water and milk ices in China and Japan, in the thirteenth century, and brought them home to Europe.

Still another bit of legend reminds us that Richard the Lion-Hearted of England once was sent a frozen sherbet from Saladin, the leader of Mohammedan armies.

There also seems to be proof that early in the seventeenth century, ice cream was served in Parisian cafes. A man by the name of Procope Cultelli, a confectioner from Florence, Italy, who went to Paris in 1660, and there opened a cafe, among other things served ice cream dishes.

There is yet another legend which concerns a French chef named Gerlad Tissain, who was supposed to have invented ice cream in the year 1640. When he first introduced it to Charles I, he received a reward of a life pension of £20. What Tissain actually did was to improve the water ices served at the famous banquets of Catherine de Medici. The story goes on to say that when Charles I lost his head, Tissain lost his pension and then sold his secret recipe to the Café Neapolitan in Paris.

132.   Ice Cream Cone

It was at the St. Louis World's Fair in 1904 that that the ice cream cone made its first appearance. A Syrian gentleman named Hamwi had come from Damascus to sell *zalabia* at the fair. His immediate neighbor on the midway, who dispensed ice cream, one day ran out of clean dishes and Hamwi is supposed to have rolled his still soft *zalabia* into a cornucopia, which the ice cream vendor filled with his product and handed to a customer. Success was instantaneous. When Hamwi died in 1943, he was heading the enormously successful Western Cone Company.

133. Ice Cream Soda

This fountain beverage did not come into being until about 1874. Credit is given to one Ralph Green for having concocted it. It was at the Franklin Institute Exhibit of that year, where Green had a concession, that he served, among other things, *iced* cream soda in which he used sweet cream. As the supply of sweet cream did not last, he obtained two pitchers of ice cream from a nearby confectioner, allowing it to melt before putting it to use. To this he added some syrup and soda and thus was born the ice cream soda.

134. Ice Cream Sundae

Evanston, Illinois, the home of Frances Willard and the Woman's Christian Temperance Union (W.C.T.U.), was so Methodist-minded and pious that the city fathers passed an ordinance forbidding the sale of ice cream sodas on Sunday. Some ingenious confectioners, meaning to observe the law, served the ice cream with syrup alone and without adding soda. This became known as the sodaless soda being served on Sundays. It was so popular that orders for "Sundays" crossed the counter every day of the week. The story goes that objection was raised to naming the dish after the Sabbath Day, and accordingly the spelling was changed to "sundae."

135. I'm from Missouri

William Duncan Vandiver, a representative in Congress from the State of Missouri, while a member of the House committee on naval affairs, and while speaking at a banquet in 1899, had this to say: "I come from a state that raises corn and cotton and cockleburs and Democrats, and frothy eloquence neither convinces nor satisfies me. I am from Missouri. You have got to show me." Thus was born the phrase "I'm from Missouri."

136. Income Tax (Federal)

The sixteenth amendment to the Constitution, legalizing federal income taxes, was adopted in 1913. It began as an amendment to a bill in Congress lowering the tariff on imports. The idea was that the small deficit from reduced tariff receipts could be taken care of by a tiny tax on prosperous incomes.

On incomes from $4,000 to $20,000, the bite was one percent. Few made over $4,000. That amount had a buying power of at least $10,000 of today's money. Few opposed the idea. It didn't seem important.

137. Indian Giver

This term dates back to Colonial times. In those days the Indians apparently expected an equivalent for a gift and if they did not get one, they demanded the return of the gift.

138. Indian Summer

The name given to the mild and pleasant weather late in autumn is Indian summer. While this name had gained broad use by 1830, its origin is almost as hazy as the weather it describes. Some explanations are that the Indians predicted such spells of weather; that the smokiness in the air was produced by Indian fires; and that the season takes on the Indian character of deceptiveness.

139. Infantry

Boys on foot (mere babes in arms) once attended knights on horseback until they, too, could win their spurs. Thus the name came to be applied to foot soldiers.

140. Inferiority Complex

This phrase was first used by the famous psychoanalyst, Dr. Alfred Adler, who referred to it as "the golden complex" because of the fact that so many persons who suffered serious feelings of inferiority became outstandingly successful by overcompensating for their feelings of inferiority and becoming far more successful than would have been possible had they always felt perfectly competent and secure.

141. Installment Credit

In primitive form installment credit existed thousands of years ago. It was practiced by the Babylonians and Phoenicians. It was known in Rome under Julius Caesar, especially in real estate dealings.

Apparently the plan was imported to England early in the nineteenth century, when the Countess of Blessington found it practiced by merchants in Paris. When she returned to London, she told cabinetmakers about it.

142. Iron Curtain

The phrase was first used by Winston Churchill in a foreign affairs debate shortly after the Potsdam Conference in 1945. He described the difficulty of obtaining any reliable information about what was happening in Eastern Europe because of the iron curtain, which had divided the Continent. He used the phrase again a few months later in 1946 in his famous speech at Fulton, Missouri, when, with the President of the United States in his audience, he urged Anglo-American solidarity against the new danger arising from Soviet domination of Eastern Europe.

There are others who claim that the phrase was originated by Mrs. Ethel Snowden, who later became Lady Snowden, wife of Viscount Snowden, who was Chancellor of the Exchequer, in 1924. In her book, *Through Bolshevik Russia,* she had the line "We are behind the Iron Curtain at last."

143. It's a Long Time Between Drinks

It was not the Governor of North Carolina who said to the Governor of South Carolina: "It's a long time between drinks."

Martin I. J. Griffin, historian of the American-Irish Historical Society, spent many years digging up the facts and finally determined that the pleasantry passed between Judge Aedanus Burke, of South Carolina, and his cousin, Governor Thomas Burke, of North Carolina.

Judge Burke was never a governor, but he was a member of the first Congress. He battled consistently against any enlargement of the general powers of the Government. He died March 30, 1802.

Judge Burke was on his deathbed when his physician decided to tap him. Much water was removed. The dying Burke opened his eyes and asked where the water came from.

"From you," said the doctor.

"Impossible," declared Burke. "I never drank that much water in my whole life!"

144. Jack-o'-Lantern

Ireland has a story about the origin of the Jack-o'-lanterns carried at Hallowe'en. It seems that a stingy man named Jack was barred from heaven because of his penuriousness and forbidden to enter Hades because of his practical jokes about Satan. So he was condemned to walk the earth with his lantern until Judgment Day.

145. Jackpot

This is a term used in the game of draw-poker and describes the pot (accumulation of money staked by players), which cannot be opened until a player has a pair of jacks or better.

146. Jailbird

In early jails, prisoners were kept enclosed behind bars in what resembled birdcages. The object of this was to exhibit wrongdoers so that they might serve as examples for other people. It followed naturally that they began to be called jailbirds.

147. Jalopy

The exact origin of this term is not known but during the 1900's Mexico was a good market for used automobiles—the town of Jalapa in particular. Any old rickety car that couldn't be sold in the United States was shipped across the border. Soon all used cars were referred to as jalopies, especially the Model T Ford.

148. Jazz

This name is given to irregular rhythm in music. Its origin seems to be somewhat hazy and uncertain. One account describes it as an adaptation of Razz, the name of a band conductor in New Orleans in the year 1904.

Another account indicates that it long has been a common word used by Negroes on the Barbary Coast where it meant "to mess 'em up, and lay it on thick."

Yet a third version tells us that on October 6, 1917, an editor of the *Literary Digest* commented: "A strange word has gained widespread use in the ranks of our producers of popular music. It is 'jazz' and is used mainly as an adjective descriptive of a band. The group that plays for dancing seems infected with the virus that they try to instill as a stimulus in others. They shake and jump and writhe in ways to suggest a return to the medieval jumping mania."

149. Jeep

This name is said to have been given by a private soldier of the United States Army to an exceedingly powerful, open, small, high motor car of a general utility model. Perhaps the letters "G.P." (general purposes) painted on the sides inspired the name of jeep.

150. Jew's Harp

A probable corruption of the words "jaw's harp," or "juice harp," is the most likely origin of this name. It appears to have no relation to the Jews and probably was never used by them as a musical instrument.

151. Jockey

This name as applied to the rider of horses comes from Scotland, where *Jock* is the diminutive form of John or Jack. It is also used to describe a servant. The first jockeys engaged in horse racing were boys, hence the term.

152. John Bull

This well-known collective name of the English nation was first used in Arbuthnot's satire, *The History of John Bull,* in which the French are designated as Lewis Baboon, the Dutch as Nicholas Frog, etc. *The History of John Bull* was designed to ridicule the Duke of Marlborough.

153. Jubilee

This word, as we now know it, stems from the Hebrew word *yobel,* meaning "a ram's horn blown at the beginning of the Jewish New Year."

154. Jury

The petit jury of twelve, as we know it today, is believed to show the influence of astrology. Court astrologers selected jurors, each born under a different sign of the zodiac, with the thought that by so doing they would bring to bear, upon the jury's deliberation, every type of mind.

155. Kehillah

The expression comes from a Biblical root meaning "to assemble." It is the popular name given to the Jewish communities of Lithuania, Poland and Russia which enjoyed some form of autonomous local government. Some form of this type of community was also known in Western Europe in medieval times. With autonomy practically disappearing in modern times, the term Kehillah remained as a general term for the Jewish community—no matter what form this social structure would take.

156. Kissing

The origin of kissing seems to be lost in a variety of legendary material. Among the ancient Romans matrons and virgins, the use of wine was unknown and the women were taxed with immodesty whose breath smelled of the grape. Pliny tells us that Cato was of the opinion that kissing first began between kinsmen and kinswomen, that they might know whether their wives, daughters or nieces had tasted of wine.

Some more recent scientists contend that kissing started simply as a result of a craving for salt. They seem to have discovered that the caveman could cool off in the hot summer by licking his neighbor's cheeks. From this it was a short step and more fun to be kissing one's neighbor if she happened to be a female. As years went on, the idea of thirst and salt seem to have disappeared entirely.

157. Ku Klux Klan

The secret society which grew up in some areas of southern United States about 1866 was known as the Ku Klux Klan. Its activities were directed mainly against Negroes. An act of Congress in 1871 suspended it, but it was still in evidence as an underground movement forty years later. Its victims were marked with the letters "K K K" on their foreheads. It is said that the name was taken as spelling the sound of the cocking of a gun, which was the society's principal method of murder.

158. Labor Day

As we know it, Labor Day in the United States grew out of September parades held in New York City by the Knights of Labor in the early 1880's. The first state to establish Labor Day as a legal holiday was the State of Oregon, which in 1887 set aside the first Saturday in June as Labor Day. Later in the same year the states of Colorado, New Jersey, New York, and Massachusetts followed suit and set the day as the first Monday in September. In 1894, Congress declared the day to be a national holiday.

The aim of Labor Day originally was to remind people that the fruits of industry were the product of brawn as well as brain, and of labor as well as of capital. Today it seems to be the day that marks the end of the summer vacation period.

159. Lame Duck

This epithet of disapprobation has lost much of its meaning in the United States since adoption of the 20th Amendment to the Constitution, February 6, 1933, changing the beginning of the congressional term from March 4 to January 3. Formerly there was a session of Congress between election day and the beginning of a new term, and a congressman, failing of re-election, had great difficulty bringing himself to more than a half-hearted interest in his work. Lame Duck, to the Englishman, still means one who has been crippled on the stock exchange, a defaulter, unable to discharge his obligations.

160. Leap Year

The custom of ladies proposing during Leap Year originated in the following manner:

"St. Patrick, having driven the frogs out of the bogs, was walking along the shores of Lough Neagh, when he was accosted by St. Bridget in tears, and was told that a mutiny had broken out in the nunnery over which she presided, the ladies claiming the right of 'popping the question.' St. Patrick said he would concede them the right every seventh year, when St. Bridget threw her arms around his neck, and exclaimed, 'Arrah, Patrick, jewel, I daurn't go back to the girls wid such a proposal. Make it one year in four.' St. Patrick replied, 'Bridget, Acushla, squeeze me that way again, and I'll give ye leap-year, the longest of the lot.' St. Bridget, upon this, popped the question to St. Patrick himself who, of course, could not marry; so he patched up the difficulty as best he could with a kiss and a silk gown."

In 1288, an act of the Scottish parliament permitted a lady to propose to a man and, if rejected, required that the man pay one hundred pounds unless he could show he was engaged to marry another woman.

A few years later a similar law was passed in France. Then in the fifteenth century, the tradition was legalized in Italy. By 1600 the custom had become a part of the common law of England.

161. Leathernecks

This name, as applied to men of the United States Marine Corps, seems to have come from a black leather stock issued as part of the early uniform. It was worn to keep a fighter from getting his throat slit by the whistling sweep of a snickersnee.

162. Levis

The word Levis, the term applied to a form of cowboy pants, came into being as a synonym for overalls simply because Levi Strauss and Company, of San Francisco, was the West's pioneer overall manufacturer. The first pair, so the story goes, was made out of canvas which the founder of the company had intended for wagon covers and tents. But when he discovered that gold miners of the 50's needed a garment which would stand up under the punishment of their daily labors, he quickly changed his plans. The copper rivets, added as a trademark, came about as a result of miners complaining that the gold nuggets they carried about with them were causing their pockets to rip.

163.   Life Insurance

When in the year 1583 one Richard Martin, of London, made a wager with a syndicate of thirteen English merchants that William Gybbons would not die before a specified time, he then and there became the parent of what we now know as life insurance.

164.   Lobbyist

A person who tries to get laws passed favoring a special-interest group is known as a lobbyist. The name derives from the fact that lobbyists spent their time in lobbies of various legislatures trying to talk to legislators and influence their votes.

165.   Marathon Race

The marathon race, one of the events of modern Olympic games, commemorates the reputed feat of Pheidippides, who is said to have run more than 20 miles to Athens with news of the Greek victory at Marathon in 490 B.C. According to legend, Pheidippides ran into the Athenian market place, gasped out his news, and fell dead. The Olympic marathon at present is an outdoor road race, standardized at 26 miles, 385 yards.

166.   Marriage Knot

As used in the English language, this term has only a symbolic and not a literal significance. However, in the Hindu rite, the bridegroom knots a ribbon about the neck of his bride. Before the knot is thus tied, the father of the bride may refuse his consent but not after.

Among the Parsees, the hand of the bridegroom is bound with a seven-fold knot. The Carthaginians made it a practice to tie with leather the thumbs of the couple being married, and the Romans had a custom wherein the bridegroom on the marriage day loosened the bride's belt. Even in modern times at certain gypsy weddings, the hands of the couple being married are tied or bound together.

167. Mason-Dixon Line

In popular United States parlance, the Mason-Dixon boundary divides North from South—an assumption based largely on the mistaken belief that during the Civil War it separated the Confederate states from the Union states.

The line was drawn to end an early colonial land dispute. It extends, from east to west, between Pennsylvania and Maryland, with a shorter branch reaching southward between Maryland and Delaware. All three states were on the Union side.

The Mason-Dixon line was named for two English surveyors, Charles Mason and Jeremiah Dixon, says the National Geographic Society. Skilled mathematicians and astronomers, they were invited to the American colonies in 1763 to mark the boundary finally agreed upon by long feuding proprietors and heirs of Maryland and Pennsylvania land grants.

168. Memorial Day

That day set apart each year, first by custom and later by statute, for the purpose of honoring the memory of the soldiers who fought in the Civil War, is a successor to Decoration Day which originated with the southern states when flowers were strewn over the soldiers' graves. After hostilities between the Union and Confederate forces had ceased, the widows and friends of the slain southerners showed their sincere love and gratitude to their fallen heroes in this fashion. This was not confined to Confederate graves only. These fine women of the South also decorated the graves of the northern dead. The news of this touching tribute flashed across the North as a ray of new light and hope for brotherhood, and in 1868, General John A. Logan, then Commander in Chief of the Grand Army of the Republic, showed his deep admiration of this symbolic custom by issuing an order designating May 30th of that year as the one on which all posts of the G.A.R. should commemorate the dead of the Civil War by decorating their graves with floral bouquets and wreaths. Action was soon taken by the legislatures of the various states and the 30th of May was set aside for that purpose in the majority of states.

169. Miss America Pageant

The Miss America pageant, which began in 1921, had its origin in the floral parade held in 1902. The parade was made up of rolling chairs decorated with flowers, with a girl in each chair. However, only the beauty of the decorated chairs, and not that of the girls, was judged.

170. Mistletoe

The generally accepted version of the origin of the mistletoe relates to the ancient Druid days when the sacred mistletoe was cut with a golden knife and given to the people as charms. It was hung over their doors and it was believed that only joy and happiness could enter as long as the plant remained fresh and green. In Norse mythology, mistletoe was said to bring happiness, safety, and good fortune as long as it did not touch the ground.

When Christmas was established, mistletoe became a festive decoration, but soon was banished from the churches because of the privileges of kissing which went with it, and holly became its substitute.

Yet another version of its origin tells us that Balder, the Scandinavian Apollo, had been charmed by his mother against all injuries from fire, water, air, and earth. But his ancient enemy, Loki, the bad one, made an arrow out of mistletoe. Being a parasite, it did not spring from any of the above elements. Balder was severely wounded by the mistletoe weapon, and was brought back to health only by the efforts of all the gods. Balder's mother decreed that the mistletoe plant should never again be used as a weapon. She was so grateful for her son's recovery that she promised to kiss anyone who passed beneath the branch of mistletoe.

171. Mother's Day

To Miss Anna Jarvis of Philadelphia goes the credit for inspiring national recognition of a day set aside for veneration of mothers and motherhood. Her mother had been an active worker in the church and community affairs of the small Virginia town where she spent her entire life.

In the early 1900's, shortly after her mother's death, she was asked to arrange a special memorial service in the church her mother had attended. Realizing the universal beauty of the idea, Miss Jarvis brought her experience to the attention of the church people in Philadelphia where she lived. On the second Sunday in May, 1908, the churches of that city observed their first Mother's Day services. These services were so widely acclaimed that she quietly but persistently campaigned for nationwide observance. Through her persuasion, Senator Burkett of Nebraska introduced a bill into Congress designating the second Sunday in May—the day on which Mrs. Jarvis was born—as a national Mother's Day. In May, 1914, the bill passed and it was President Wilson who signed the bill making it law, and it was he who proclaimed May 9, 1914, as the first Mother's Day.

172. Mugwump

This word was borrowed from the Indians by our New England pioneers. It originally meant "big chief" or the "head of all," and came to be applied to members of a political party who refused to follow certain dicta and whose vote could not be relied upon.

173. Nemesis

This word comes to us from the Greek word which means "to give what is due." In Greek mythology, Nemesis was the goddess who doled out to men their exact share of good or bad fortune and was responsible for seeing that everyone got his just dues and deserts.

174. News

Early newspapers printed a sign at the top of the first page of every issue indicating the four points of the compass. This implied that the information printed came from the north, east, west, and south. Later this sign was simplified until it appeared as "N–E–W–S." So now we have the word news, meaning "the latest information from the four corners of the globe."

175. Newspaper

Students of Egyptology assert that the first newspaper in the world was a clay representation of a scarab, made and circulated in Egypt in 1450 B.C. and containing carved lettering. However, the first newspaper of which we are historically certain was the *Acta Publica,* in the form of clay tablets, begun by Julius Caesar in 58 B.C. Today the oldest of printed newspapers is *The Peking News,* which began publication 950 years before the invention of printing from movable type. It is now well over 1,400 years old.

The newspaper in its modern form usually is regarded as beginning in 1566, when the government of Venice, Italy, issued written news-sheets and exhibited them in the streets. Anyone was allowed to read them on payment of a small coin called a *gazetta.* On this account the news-sheets were called gazettes, and they became so popular they were printed. Soon after the date mentioned, gazettes were issued in most of the big cities of Europe. The first English newspaper was the *Weekly News,* published in London in 1622. But in this paper and its successors down to 1641 only foreign news was printed.

176. Nisei

This term which came to be applied to loyal, American-born Japanese during World War II, means "second generation." It comes from the Japanese word *sei,* meaning "generation." *Is, ni, sen* mean "one," "two," "three." Thus the first generation to come to the United States are *issei;* their sons *nisei;* and their grandsons *sensei.*

177. Nylon

As the story goes, the term nylon was given to a product created by its inventor, who worked on developing it both in New York and London. By taking the first letters of New York and combining it with the first three letters of London, one gets the word nylon.

178. O.K.

The following editorial, which appeared in the *Chicago Tribune* on December 4, 1962, seems to give us the latest word on the expression O.K.:

"The battle over the origin of the expression 'O.K.' which supposedly was settled 21 years ago, has erupted again.

"It was in 1941 that Allen Walker Read traced the earliest appearance of the expression to a New York newspaper of March 23, 1840, reporting the formation of the Democratic O.K. club, an organization dedicated to the reëlection of President Van Buren. Van Buren was born in Kinderhook, New York, hence, according to Mr. Read, the nickname Old Kinderhook and hence, in turn, the initials. The late Henry L. Mencken accepted this as a 'sound and dramatic' end to the long battle, and the Old Kinderhook theory has been widely accepted.

"Ironically, it is the same Mr. Read, now professor of English at Columbia, who has upset his own theory. He has discovered an 'O.K.' in the Boston *Morning Post* of March 23, 1839, exactly a year earlier than the New York article.

"The Boston story had to do with a dispute over the ringing of dinner bells. The leader of one faction, it is said, 'would have had the "contribution box," et ceteras, o.k.—all correct—and cause the corks to fly, like sparks, upward.'

"Whatever was meant by this sentence, it clearly had nothing to do with Van Buren, Old Kinderhook, or politics. Professor Read therefore reverts to an earlier theory that O.K. stood for 'oll korrect.' To support this, he points out that O.W., standing for 'oll wright,' had already been popular in Boston. The 'oll korrect' theory is one of ten which Mencken had advanced before accepting Professor Read's.

"We must admit that the Old Kinderhook theory was an inviting one. It avoided the suggestion that Bostonians couldn't spell, and it also flattered the New York politicians. But for once Mr. Mencken may have been too kind. As it looks now, the Bostonians will be remembered as poor spellers and the New York politicians as opportunists who probably coined the nickname Old Kinderhook just to take advantage of the initials which were already popular—a practice which is not uncommon even today."

179. Olympic Games

Legend has it that the Olympic Festival began as a celebration of Zeus' victory over Kronos when they wrestled for control of the world. History states that the Olympic games began in 776 B.C. with a foot race on the plains of Olympia beside the River Alpheus. The winner was a cook named Coroebus from nearby Elis and his reward a wild olive wreath.

180. Oscar

The gold statuette, symbolic of the Motion Picture Academy Awards, was given its name by Mrs. Margaret Herrick in 1931. She was then executive secretary of the Academy. Studying the figure, she remarked that it had the square jaw and sharp features of an uncle who happened to be named Oscar. Bette Davis and other movie stars referred to the trophy as Oscar and the name stuck.

181. Ouija Board

Table tapping, a form of foretelling future events, was practiced by the ancient Persians, Greeks, and Romans. Marcellinus, a Roman historian, writes of a certain Hilarius who was imprisoned in 378 for using some such method to predict the successor to Emperor Valens. The ouija board, while similar in concept, is of comparatively recent origin —the 1890's. It consists of two pieces: a smoothly finished board printed with letters of the alphabet and mystic symbols; and a small heart-shaped table with three legs, called a *planchette,* which is placed on the board. Then two or more persons gather around and rest their fingers lightly on the *planchette.* Without being guided, the little table is then supposed to move from letter to letter, spelling out words and sentences, foretelling future events. Ouija, the name, comes from a combination of the French and German words for "yes."

182. Paper Money

Back in the Middle Ages, when travel by varied conveyances became common, metal coins, especially gold, were looked on by most as a burden. Travelers were easy prey for highwaymen, and this led to the wayfarer's leaving his coins with a goldsmith, who in turn gave the depositor a receipt, which was accepted along the way for fares and purchases.

This custom grew with time and gradually the receipts were transferred from one person to another for payment of debts. This, in effect, was the beginning of paper money at work.

Paper money, as we know it today in the United States, was the result of a financial crisis during the Civil War. The nation was using metal money almost exclusively, and President Abraham Lincoln couldn't get enough of it to pay the troops. Some of his advisers urged him to print paper money and he sent them to confer with Treasury Secretary Salmon P. Chase, who informed them angrily that such a scheme was unconstitutional. Next day Lincoln sent the men back to Chase carrying this note: "You take care of the money in the Treasury and I will take care of the Constitution." Paper money, or "greenbacks" as they were then called, have been with us ever since.

183. Pastor

This title, which we use interchangeably with preacher and minister, originally meant shepherd.

184. Pawnshop

What is said to be the first public pawnshop was founded in 1462 by a Franciscan friar, Bernardino de Feltre of Perugia, Italy. Its purpose was charitable and thus it gained the Church's approval.

A needy person could obtain a loan by leaving some article as collateral. When redeeming the article he paid back what he had borrowed plus an additional 15% for upkeep of the shop.

In Perugia today, the successor to this first Monte di Pieta (Mountain of Pity) still flourishes under the name Banco di Credito e Pegno (Bank of Credit and Pledge). It is thought to be the oldest continuous banking service in the world.

185. Perfume

Literally *par fume,* meaning "through smoke," and probably extending back to primitive times when the only perfume the caveman knew was released by burning woods and gums.

186. Phi Beta Kappa

This honorary scholastic fraternity was founded December 5, 1776, by fifty men at the College of William and Mary in Williamsburg, Virginia. The Greek letters *phi, beta* and *kappa* are the initials of the Greek words meaning "Philosophy, the Guide of Life." Membership in this fraternity results from persons being elected by vote of college faculty members among senior and junior college students with the best academic records.

187. Philadelphia Lawyer

This term meaning "a very shrewd lawyer," is a tribute to the high reputation of the Philadelphia bar in Colonial times. In 1788 the *Universal Asylum and Columbia Magazine,* published in London, printed this sentence: "In speaking of a difficult point, they say 'it would puzzle a Philadelphia lawyer.'"

The phrase "sharp as a Philadelphia lawyer" seems to date from the trial of John Peter Zenger for libeling the British Governor William Cosby, back in August of 1735. Andrew Hamilton, who hailed from Philadelphia, won his case by his eloquence and audacity, and as his fame for superiority in legal skill spread throughout the world, it brought fame to the phrase "Philadelphia lawyer."

188. Pin-Money

This term is applied to a lady's allowance of money for her own personal expenditure. Immediately after the invention of pins, in the fourteenth century, they were very costly and the maker was allowed to sell them in open shop only on the 1st and 2nd of January. It was then that the ladies of the court and the city dames flocked to the stores to buy them, having first been provided with the requisite money by their husbands. When pins became common and cheap, the ladies spent their allowances on other fancies, but the term "pin-money" remained.

189. Playing Cards

Present-day playing cards were designed in 1392 by Jack Gringonneur, court painter to Charles VI of France. He founded his pack on a regular system. A pack consists of fifty-two cards, the number of weeks in a year; there are thirteen cards to a suit, the number of lunar months. The four suits represent the four social classes of Gringonneur's time. Spades were for the pikemen or soldiery; clubs were designed as a cloverleaf, the emblem of husbandry; diamonds represented the diamond-shaped hat of the artisan; and hearts came from the French word *coeur,* an evolution from *Chorur,* meaning "the clergy." The first cards used in the United States were brought by the Spanish to their early settlements.

190. Poinsettia

This Christmas flower of the Southland gets its name from the man who introduced it, Joel R. Poinsett of South Carolina.

191. Poolroom

Originally a poolroom was a place in which lottery tickets were sold. Lottery, because of the manner in which winnings were paid off, was called "pool." Since lottery tickets were sold all day and the drawings were not held until late in the evening, proprietors of poolrooms installed billiard tables to occupy their customers during the long waiting periods. The game of billiards was either too slow or too difficult for the hangers-on. They devised a game of their own, first called "pocket billiards" and later "pool."

192. Post Cards

Post cards originated in Austria on October 1, 1869. Exactly one year later they were offered in England. Francis Kilvert, a young Anglican curate, wrote the following in his diary for October 4, 1870: "Today I sent my first post cards . . . They are capital things, simple, useful, and handy. A happy invention." The first English cards were court size (3½ × 4½ inches), and only official ones were allowed. Private cards were introduced in 1894; later, picture cards.

193. Potter's Field

We have at least two legends relating to the origin of this term. According to one, potter's field is a piece of ground, usually adjoining a cemetery, reserved for the burying of friendless poor and strangers. The name is derived from a Biblical phrase. The gospel according to St. Matthew 27:7 relates that after Judas was condemned he took back to the chief priests and elders the 30 pieces of silver. They took counsel and bought with them the potter's field, in which to bury strangers.

According to the second version, ancient Babylonian serfs worked in fields gathering clay for bricks and pottery. When one died he was buried without ceremony in a hole from which he himself had removed the clay.

194. Pretzel

Once upon a time in the monasteries in southern France (or according to some versions northern Italy), children were rewarded with gifts when they had learned to say their prayers correctly. A monk in the year 610 A.D. made the first pretzel to give to the youngsters. He designed the twist peculiar alone to the pretzel to represent arms folded in the attitude of prayer. In Latin he called it *pretiola*, meaning "little gift." News of the delicious taste of the wholesome, rich brown pretzels spread rapidly and the "little gifts" soon became known and enjoyed by people all over the world.

195. Primary Election

In 1899, Minnesota passed a primary election law which applied to candidates for city and county offices, judges and elective members of school, library and park boards in counties having populations of 200,000 or more. Hennepin County was the only one that had the required population when the law went into effect. The Wisconsin primary law passed four years later, in 1903, had no limitation in its application with respect to population of counties. The first Wisconsin primary election was held in 1906, and the first governor nominated and subsequently elected was James Ole Davidson.

196. Printer's Devil

Take your choice! According to one legend this phrase is one which is lovingly applied to a boy-of-all-work around a printing office—probably stemming from the usual inky blackness of this scamp. Then, too, there being an aura of mystery surrounding the art of the early printer, ignorant townspeople were wont to link him with supernatural forces. There also is the story about William Caxton employing an apprentice of French descent named de Ville.

According to another version, Aldus Manutius (1449–1515), the celebrated Venetian printer and publisher, had a small black slave whom the superstitious believed to be an emissary of Satan. To satisfy the curious, one day he said publicly in church "I, Aldus Manutius, printer to the Holy Church, have this day made public exposure of the printer's devil. All who think he is not flesh and blood, come and pinch him." Hence in Venice arose the somewhat curious sobriquet of the "printer's devil."

197. Quack

This word is an abbreviation of the seventeenth century Dutch *quacksalver*, meaning a medical charlatan or a maker of ointment who boasts, or quacks, about the superlative virtue of his own product without knowing anything about medicine or its practice. Like the duck, the quack is one who makes a big noise over nothing.

198. Rabbi

This title, given to those who are designated as spiritual leaders of the Jewish communities, is derived from a Hebrew noun "Rab." In biblical Hebrew the noun meant "great or distinguished." Thus "Rabbi" might be translated as "my great one" or "more" indicating that the individual so designated had "much" or "more" learning. In post-Biblical Hebrew the term "Rab" came to mean "master" (in contradistinction to "slave"). Thus the expression "Rabbi" has often been translated literally as "my master." This title was not known before the first century of the Common Era. The first to have been given this title is claimed to be Rabbi Gamliel the elder. This form of the title, "Rabban," was given only to the head of the Sanhedrin (i.e., "our master"). The title "Rabbi" (my master) is said to have been first used by the disciples of Rabbi Johanan ben Zakkai. In general the title was indicative of ordination enabling its bearer to pass judgment, either originally as a member of the Sanhedrin, or later as a member of an academy of learning or as a spiritual leader of a community.

199. Rabbit's Foot

This symbol for good luck should be useful to the rabbit—he has four, and he needs all of them when hunting dogs are hot on his trail. It originated as a good luck symbol in show business where it was used as a powder puff in makeup, and when lost or misplaced, it might delay a performance . . . bad luck. Hence, the reverse when it wasn't.

200. Radar

The name for this military device comes from the first letters of the unabbreviated name which describes its function—Radio Detection and Ranging.

201. Red Tape

Charles Dickens is responsible for this expression. Governmental departments in Dickens' time were notoriously slow. They tied their documents with red tape. He was the first one to apply this term to slow methods of handling business.

202. Robot

This term is synonymous with automation. It was popularized in the 1920's when the Czech playwright Karel Capek brought his play, "R.U.R." to the United States. These initials stand for Rossum's Universal Robots, a firm manufacturing mechanical men. The word "robot" stems from the Czech word *robotnik,* which means "slave," which in turn comes from *robota,* which means "to work."

203. Roorback

When James K. Polk was a candidate for the presidency of the United States, those opposing him gave widespread publicity to a purported book by a mythical Baron von Roorbach (sometimes Roorback), in which certain unsavory practices involving Polk were said to have been described. The falsity of these allegations was soon exposed. As a carry-over into the present any untruth, particularly when told during the course of a political campaign or for political advantage, is still referred to as a roorback.

204. Rubber Heel

The popular heel that has been a blessing to foot comfort and shock resistance in walking was invented by accident. A printer named Humphrey O'Sullivan had sore feet that ached and fatigued him as he worked at his machine. One day he got the bright idea of placing a resilient rubber mat on the floor in front of the machine. This gave his feet much comfort. But his fellow workers, as a practical joke, would hide the rubber mat from him. Necessity being the mother of invention, O'Sullivan countered with an idea. Why not nail a piece of rubber mat to his shoes? And so was born the rubber heel.

205. Russian Roulette

The most dangerous gambling game ever played is called "Russian Roulette." The odds are always 5 to 1 in your favor but . . . Soldiers in the Russian army started it when they became bored with service on some far-flung frontier where nothing ever happened. One bullet was put into a six-shooter, the barrel was then spun, the soldier would put the revolver to his temple and press the trigger. The chances are 5 to 1 there would be a click and no explosion. After a wave of "suicides" Russian intelligence officers tracked down the cause and from then on a soldier playing this game was open to court martial on the only charge brass hats could figure out—"wasting ammunition."

206. St. Valentine's Day

The custom of sending declarations of love on St. Valentine's Day began in medieval France and England. The popular belief was that birds began to pair February 14, which made it a proper occasion for sending lovers' tokens. The tokens took their name from the saint of the day, a third-century priest named Valentine.

207. Salt-Spilling

The superstition which attaches to the spilling of salt as a sign of bad luck seems to come from the painting of the Last Supper, by Leonardo da Vinci, in which Judas is depicted as spilling salt on the table.

208. Salvation Army

William Booth, a Methodist minister, with the help of his wife, Catherine, organized the Salvation Army. Booth began as an independent evangelist working in Cornwall, England, about the year 1861. Shortly thereafter he moved to London where he began holding outdoor meetings. The movement was then known as the East London

Revival Society and later called the Christian Mission. It acquired the designation as Salvation Army in 1878 and was organized along military lines, its evangelists carrying the activities into the field of social welfare and attracting world-wide attention. The story goes that Booth said that his Mission was a salvation army, thus inspiring the present-day name and setup of the organization.

209. Sandwich

It was during the reign of King George III that what we now know as a sandwich was named after the Earl of Sandwich. He was supposed to have been so great a gambler that he could not wait to eat his meals, but instead took his food in this form so that he would not lose any time while he continued his play. While originally sandwiches consisted solely of meat and bread, nowadays they take on many different forms.

210. Santa Claus

This name would seem to be a German corruption of St. Nicholas, a fourth-century bishop who died in the year 352 A.D. His birthday was long celebrated on December 6 in Europe. Legend has it that on the evening of that day he made his tour, visiting palace and cottage alike, the children placed stockings or other receptacles for the gifts which he was expected to drop down to them through the chimneys of their homes. The Dutch brought the custom to New Amsterdam and called him *Sinter Klaas*, which in English became Santa Claus.

Dr. Clement Clarke Moore of New York, in a famous poem entitled *A Visit from St. Nicholas*, first published in December, 1823, put the Santa Claus myth in the form we now accept in this country. It was he who invented the sleigh and the reindeer and all else that goes with it, Dasher, Dancer, Prancer, Vixen, Comet, Cupid, Donner, and Blitzen.

211. Sausage

One of the oldest forms of preserved foods, sausages antedate recorded history, and the art of sausage-making probably developed slowly from the process of salting and drying meats as a means of preserving them. The relatively modern word sausage is a derivative of the Latin *salsus*, meaning "salted."

By the Middle Ages, sausage-making had become an art practiced commercially in many localities. The skins of casings used were hog, sheep, and beef gut, and referred to as natural casings; while these are still being used in the manufacture of sausage, synthetic vegetable compounds are being more and more substituted as casings.

212. Scapegoat

This word comes from ancient times when on Yom Kippur, the Jewish Day of Atonement, Aaron laid the sins of the people on the head of a goat and sent it into the wilderness. At the same time that this was going on, a second goat was sacrificed to the Lord. Thus it is that the modern scapegoat means "one who is made to bear the blame for another."

213. Scotland Yard

England's Scotland Yard got its name because its London site once was occupied by a palace belonging to the Kings of Scotland.

214. Scuttlebutt

This is navy language for "gossip." It is derived from the word *butt,* meaning "cask," and the word *scuttle,* meaning "hole." The scuttle-butt stood on the deck of old sailing vessels and served as a source of daily water supply. It was there the men gathered for a drink and to exchange gossip.

215. Serendipity

This word means the ability to make unexpected or lucky discoveries. It was coined by Horace Walpole, who formed it from the title of a fairy story, *The Three Princes of Serendip,* because the princes were always finding things of which they were not in quest.

216. Shill

An accomplice used to lure suckers into sideshows to purchase gadgets and patent medicines from sidewalk peddlers, or to help the bidding at an auction. This word probably stems from the British slang word *Shillibeer,* which originally was the name of a bus service in Britain. In this regard it is well to recall that rubberneck buses were among the first users of the shill. Operators hired one or more persons to sit in their vehicles between trips to avoid giving the impression that the buses were empty and void of sightseers.

217. Siamese Twins

The name is derived from a set of twins, Chang and Eng, born of Chinese parents in Siam in 1811. The term is used to designate two nearly complete individuals united side by side or back to back. Chang and Eng were exhibited for many years in P. T. Barnum's circus, after which they settled in North Carolina, married English sisters, and had a total of 22 children. They died within two hours of each other in 1874.

218. Sirloin

There are many theories as to the origin of this word, the most popular of which tells us that a particularly choice cut of meat once appealed so strongly to an English monarch that he bestowed knighthood upon it before settling down to a feast. He dubbed the steak Sir Loin. Credit has at various times been given to Henry VII, Charles II, and James I, though it would appear the term was used long before the time of James I.

Others theorize that the word sirloin is actually an adaptation of the old French word *surlonge,* formed from *sur,* meaning "above" or "over," and *longe,* meaning "loin."

219. Smoke-Filled Room

In 1920, during the deadlock at the Republican convention, Harry M. Daugherty of Ohio made a statement to the newsmen: "The convention will be deadlocked, and after the other candidates have gone the limit, some men, worn out and bleary-eyed for lack of sleep, will sit down around a table in a smoke-filled room and decide the nomination. When that time comes, Harding will be selected."

220. Smörgåsbord

Smörgåsbord originated in Scandinavian countries as a traditional gesture of hospitality on feast days and wedding celebrations. Distances were long and travel hard, so guests sometimes stayed for two weeks. They brought an assortment of foods. These offerings were laid out on a common table for all to enjoy.

221. Snob

When commoners registered for Cambridge University it was necessary for them to place *sine nobilitate,* without nobility, after their names. This was shortened to *s. nob.* and soon became "snob," a pretender to position.

222. Soda Pop

When carbonated beverages were first put into bottles they were sealed with corks which frequently released the carbonation. To prevent this from happening, Charles G. Hutchinson invented the Hutchinson Bottle Stopper. The year, 1878. Oldtimers will remember this assembly of stout wire and rubber washer which imparted its own peculiar flavor to the beverage. Pulled up tight, the Hutchinson Bottle Stopper sealed in the carbonation, the carbonation itself holding it there. Pushed inward, the beverage could be poured or swallowed direct from the bottle. The act of pushing in the stopper resulted in a "pop"—and it is from this familiar sound that the "soda pop" of years ago took its name.

223. Sophomore

This comes to us from the Greek language. It is a combination of the word *sophos,* meaning "wise," and *moros,* meaning "fool"—the combination "wise fool" meaning one who knows enough at least to understand that he does not know everything, which would make such an attitude the beginning of true wisdom.

224. S.O.S.

In the opinion of some persons the distress signal used by ships at sea means "Save Our Ship." But the letters do not stand for words and have no meaning in themselves. They were adopted at the Radio-Telegraph Conference in 1912 because the combination of dots and dashes (three dots, three dashes, three dots) was so easy to send that the most inexperienced radio operator would have no difficulty with it.

225. Southpaw

This term used in baseball to designate a left-handed player is believed to have originated in Chicago where the team's baseball park faced west. A man who pitched left-handed in that park would be doing so with his south paw.

226. Spoonerism

William Archibald Spooner, dean and warden of New College, Oxford, gave his name, perhaps unwillingly, to the freak of speech in which letters or sounds in one word are transposed to another nearby word. The only authenticated spoonerism by the late warden occurred in New College Chapel in 1879 when he announced the hymn "Conquering Kings" as "Kinkering Congs."

227. Spooning

The term spooning has its origin in an old Welsh courting custom. A swain calling on his sweetheart was compelled to carve a set of wooden spoons to keep his hands busy.

228. Standard Time

Until the latter part of the nineteenth century, time was established in each community by a town clock set by sun reckoning or railroad train time. This caused confusion. In 1882, Congress authorized the President to call an international conference to select a common prime meridian for reckoning longitude and regulating time throughout the world. On October 1, 1884, delegates from 26 countries met in Washington. Although most of the delegates favored Greenwich, England, as the point at which to designate the prime meridian, the conference did not formally adopt this principle. In the meantime the United States and Canada had agreed on a series of time zones in multiples of 15 degrees, corresponding to one hour of sun-time difference. The zones in the United States were Eastern (75° west of Greenwich), Central (90° west), Mountain (105°), and Pacific (120°). Many communities still maintained sun time but eventually standard time was adopted.

229. Stateroom

The captain's room on an English vessel, or one set aside for royalty and government officials when traveling, circa 1650, was called the stateroom. When steamboat travel was popular on the rivers of the United States, the rooms were named for states of the union, thus permitting the common traveler to ride in his own stateroom—another American freedom. It is worthy of mention that the largest stateroom usually was called Texas.

230. Stool Pigeon

Pigeons in pioneer days were so numerous they were a menace to crops. One extermination method was to catch a pigeon and tie it to a "call stool" in a field. When other pigeons flocked around the decoy it was easy to trap them. From this practice came the expression "stool pigeon."

231. Stop—Look—Listen

This warning slogan was devised by Ralph R. Upton in 1912. He was a safety lecturer for the Puget Sound Power Company of Seattle, Washington, and wished to improve the signs then in use at railroad crossings, which read "Look Out for the Engine."

232. Straw Vote

For many decades the term "straw vote" has been used to indicate an unofficial vote of poll designed to predict the probable outcome of an election or other issue. As early as 1887 the San Francisco *Thunderbolt* reported "The straw vote taken at the Report office is unreliable." In recent years the use of polls or "straw votes" has become a factor in determining public opinion. The term takes its name from the early practice of throwing a handful of straw into the air to determine which way the wind was blowing and also from drawing straws to settle a controversy or to establish a course of action, with the decision falling to the person with the longest straw.

233. Swan Song

There was a popular belief that swans burst into beautiful song just before death. This belief has been traced to ancient times. Swans were held sacred by Apollo, the Greek god of music, and one Greek legend was that the soul of Apollo passed into a swan. A later legend, probably based on the earlier one, held that the souls of all great poets pass into swans. These legends were the basis for the figurative expression "swan song" applied at first to the final work of a poet or the last performance of a singer. Later its meaning was broadened to include any last or farewell work or performance.

Another version credits the German composer, Richard Wagner, with having created the expression when he presented his opera "Lohengrin," in which a boat drawn by a swan bears Lohengrin away from Elsa, while he sings his farewell. Thus the term "swan song" has taken on the meaning of irrevocable departure.

234. Table Tennis

The first table tennis balls probably were champagne corks. In the 1890's Mr. James Gibb, a Cambridge (England) engineer, invented the game in which the corks were knocked from one side of the table to the other with cigar box lids. A few years later the game was revolutionized when an English visitor to the United States noticed babies playing with celluloid balls. On his suggestion, these balls replaced the cork and rubber ones then in use. The game was known as ping-pong and stayed that way until 1927. Then it was changed to table tennis because ping-pong was a proprietary name belonging to a firm making equipment for the game.

235. Tabloid

This word, coined in the nineteenth century, was applied to many products in condensed and compact form. In the United States it has been applied to newspapers with pages about half the usual size.

236. Tammany Hall

The Society of Tammany, or Columbia Order, is a political organization formed in 1783 chiefly through the efforts of William Mooney, an upholsterer in New York City. The name of the society, which was not formally organized until May 12, 1789, was borrowed from the Sons of St. Tammany whose patron was Tammanend, or Tammany, a Delaware chief. In 1805, it was incorporated as a charitable organization, but its activity in politics gradually increased and by 1852 its fame as a political group was established.

237. Tank

A queer name for a heavily armored motor fort, running on caterpillar treads. It was described as a water carrier destined for Mesopotamia in army communiques so that the enemy would have no advance information of its real purpose. It was first used in World War I by the British in an attack on the German lines at Flers, September 15, 1916.

238. Taps

After the bloody fighting of the peninsula campaign during the U.S. Civil War, the weary troops of General Daniel Butterfield's brigade were camping on bluffs overlooking the James River in Virginia. As the bugler sounded "extinguish lights," General Butterfield remarked to a fellow officer, "That call sounds too formal." He had only a smattering of musical knowledge but by the next morning he had worked out a new melody for the bugler. The bugler tried it. The general made a few changes. The bugler played it again. General Butterfield nodded approvingly and ordered that it be played every night as a last call. Other brigades heard the rise and fall of the smooth, haunting melody and adopted it. This is the commonly accepted version of how "taps," derived from tattoo, a drum signal often combined with bugles, had its inception in the Army.

239. Tariff

When the Moors were masters of Spain their ships used to lie in wait for merchant vessels coming through the Straits of Gibraltar bound for Italy, Greece, and Egypt. The Moors were no fools. Instead of plundering the vessels they levied a sort of blackmail with a fixed scale of payment based on the value of the cargo . . . this was determined at their port of Tarifa. Thus originated the word tariff. Some people still think the tariff is a form of piracy after all these years of government sanction.

240. Tea Bags

Tea bags came into being when a wholesale tea merchant in New York ordered silk bags to hold samples of tea distributed to his customers. He did not realize that those customers were pouring hot water over the bags in a cup and that he had developed the tea bag.

241. Ten-Gallon Hat

It isn't a matter of Texas exaggeration or of liquid capacity—but of folk etymology. The Spaniards in the old days of the Southwest ornamented their large-brimmed hats with braid, often silver braid. Very fine hats might have had as many as five or seven or even ten of these braids. And the Spanish word for braid of this kind was *galéon*.

242. Tennis

The name of our popular game of the courts is said to be derived from the warning cry of the server: "tenetz!" This old English word, as nearly as may be determined, meant "ready" or "prepare to receive the service," probably from French *tenez*, or take. Philip Hitti, in his history *The Arabs*, suggests that tennis is from Tinnis, an Egyptian city noted in the middle ages for its linen—from which the best tennis balls were made.

243. Thanksgiving Day

The custom of celebrating a day of thanks in this country was originated by Governor Bradford of Massachusetts after the first harvest of the Pilgrims in 1621. President George Washington proclaimed November 26, 1789 to be a day of thanksgiving. In 1815, President Madison set aside a day of thanks to mark the return of peace after the War of 1812. By 1830 the State of New York had adopted a day of thanksgiving as an annual custom, and other states soon followed. In 1863, at the urging of Mrs. Sarah J. Hale, editor of *Godey's Lady's Book*, President Lincoln issued a proclamation fixing the fourth Thursday in November as Thanksgiving Day. Later, the official national Thanksgiving Day became the last Thursday in November. In 1939, President Roosevelt proclaimed November 23 to be the day of observance but many states refused to accept this and continued to use November 30. It was not until 1941 that Congress got around to fixing a national date and decreed that Thanksgiving in each year should be the third Thursday in November, which it now is.

244. Thimble

The thimble was originally called a thumb bell by the English because worn on the thumb; then it was referred to as a thumble, and finally its present name. It was a Dutch invention, and was first brought to England in 1695. Thimbles formerly were made only of iron and brass, but in comparatively late years they have been made of gold, steel, horn, ivory, and even glass and pearl. In China beautifully carved pearl thimbles are seen, bound with gold and with the end of gold. The first thimble introduced into Siam was a bridal gift from the king to the queen, it was shaped like a lotus bud, made of gold, and thickly studded with diamonds arranged to spell the queen's name.

245. Throwing Rice at the Bride

The practice of throwing rice at a young married couple is derived from the Indian practice of throwing corn over their heads. The rice or corn thrown by the Hindus is a wish for fecundity, and the bridegroom throws three handfuls over the bride and the bride does the same over the bridegroom. As we know the practice, the rice is thrown by well-meaning friends.

246. To the Bitter End

This phrase has a nautical origin. A ship's anchor chain, at the point where it was fastened to a vertical timber called the bitt, was known as the bitter end. Thus when the chain has been played out to the bitter end, there's nothing more that can be done.

247. Trading Stamps

In 1891, trading stamps were originated by Thomas Alexander Sperry of Bridgeport, Connecticut, and in 1896 he organized the Sperry & Hutchinson Company to exploit the stamps.

248. Turnpike

This word came from the early American custom of blocking toll roads with pikes or poles. When the toll fee had been duly paid, the pikes or poles were lowered or turned.

249. Tuxedo

Young gentlemen at the opening dance of the exclusive Tuxedo Club near New York in 1886, flaunted a new type of jacket, cut to their design, that has since become America's national costume for evening wear. Unwittingly, by eliminating the tails of a formal full-dress coat and thus creating the "tuxedo," they imitated the word's origin. Tuxedo comes from Algonquian Indian *p'tauk-seet*, "the bear"—an animal black and tailless.

250. Uncle Sam

This term came into use in the War of 1812 and was born at Troy, New York. The government inspector there was Uncle Sam Wilson, and when the war opened Elbert Anderson, the contractor at New York, bought a large amount of beef, pork, and pickles for the army. These were inspected by Wilson, and were duly labeled E.A.—U.S., meaning Elbert Anderson, for the United States. The term U.S. for the United States was then somewhat new, and the workmen concluded that they referred to Uncle Sam Wilson. After they discovered their mistake, they kept up the name as a joke. These same men soon went to the war. There they repeated the joke. It got into print and went the rounds. From that time on the term "Uncle Sam" was used facetiously for the United States, and it now represents the nation.

251. Undertaker

Long years ago each village had a handy man who earned his living by "undertaking" odd jobs of any kind. Laying out and embalming corpses, an undesirable task to most people, usually fell to his lot. The "handy man" has narrowed his field to embalming and burying, and prefers the more dignified title of mortician, but the original term, undertaker, still sticks around.

252. Vatican

The name of the Vatican, principal residence of the popes since their return from Avignon in 1377, is derived from its location on the Vatican hill in Rome. It originated in a residence built for Pope Symmachus between 498 and 514. It was rebuilt and greatly enlarged under Nicholas V, Sixtus IV, Alexander VI, and Julius II. Only a small part is the Sistine Chapel, on a wall of which is painted Michelangelo's immortal "Last Judgment."

253. Wall Street

The center of one of the greatest financial districts in the world, Wall Street is situated in the lower part of Manhattan Island, New York City, and extends east from Broadway to the East River. The street received its name from a stockade, or wall, which was built in 1653 by Peter Stuyvesant, Dutch colonial governor, to protect the area south of the wall from the English and the Indians.

254. Watered Stock

This term, applied to stock when the capital is increased without a like increase in assets, owes its origin to a cattle dealer in New York State. As the story goes, this dealer sold a wealthy New Yorker some cattle, but first he fed them a large quantity of salt and watered them heavily to increase their weight.

255. White Elephant

The King of Siam once made it a practice to present certain courtiers whom he disliked, or wished to ruin, with a white elephant. As the white elephant is sacred in Siam, and cannot be sold, killed or given away, the expense of keeping it usually proved disastrous to the unlucky courtier. Thus today we have the expression "white elephant" meaning "any burdensome possession."

256. White House, The

It has always been called the White House. But it was not until 1850 that the first bathtub was installed in the presidential residence. Millard Fillmore was the daring executive who took this step towards cleaner politics!

257. Windfall

Good fortune is often called a windfall. This stems from medieval England, when commoners had trouble finding wood for fuel. Royal decree prohibited them from chopping down trees, so when wind knocked down branches it was a stroke of good luck.

258. "X" (The Unknown Quantity)

The Greeks were such concrete thinkers that they didn't bother to develop an algebra with abstract "unknowns." The Egyptians hold the earliest claim to equation-writing: a manuscript of 1800 B.C. speaks of the unknown as *hau*—"heap." The Hindus did better. They used abbreviated syllables or initials of objects, but they also had plus, minus and equal signs. The sixteenth century Frenchman, Vieta, is credited with first using capital letters for unknowns. Fifty years after his death, Descartes' *Geometrie* appeared which specified that the beginning letters of the alphabet be used for given quantities, the end letters for unknowns—and so it still is done today.

259. X-Rays

Less than a century ago, William Roentgen was startled by an extraordinary event while working in a dark room. While an electric discharge passed through a tube covered with black paper, a small screen covered with barium platinocyanide several feet away gave off a strange glow. In his experiments with the penetrating ray he discovered, he placed his hand before a sensitized photographic plate. The printed film showed the bones darker than the surrounding flesh. Roentgen had taken a picture through an opaque solid. He named these rays x-rays.

260. Yankee

No definite origin can be established for this term. British soldiers first used it in contempt when referring to New Englanders. In 1758, a letter of General James Wolfe referred to troops serving under him: ". . . I can afford you two companies of Yankees." Use of the term by New Englanders cannot be found prior to the battle of Lexington (April 19, 1775). After that battle residents of New England tried to dignify the nickname by inventing a mythical tribe of Massachusetts Indians, the "Yankoes," meaning the invincibles.

There are others who claim that the Dutch are responsible indirectly for this term used to designate a New Englander or to distinguish a Northerner from a Southerner. Jan Kees, meaning "Johnny Cheese," was a Flanders nickname for Hollanders because of their love of cheese. Dutch freebooters of New York (New Amsterdam) applied, in turn, the term to English traders (cheese buyers) of Connecticut. In time Jan Kees became Yankee in much the same way that San Nicholaas became Santa Claus.

261. Zany

When a person acts foolishly or doesn't make much sense, we might say he's "zany." This word comes to us from the Italian. In Italian comic operas there often is a buffoon or fool, who mimics the clown. He is called a *zannie,* which means a buffoon and we get our word zany from this!

FIRSTS

1. Air Mail Pilot

On September 23, 1911, Earl Ovington was sworn in at Garden City, Long Island, New York, as the first United States air mail pilot.

2. Air Mail Postage Stamps

On May 13, 1918, the first air mail postage stamps were issued.

3. Air Mail Service

The first regular air mail service between New York City and Washington, D.C., was established in 1918.

4. Airplane Flight

The Wright Brothers made their first flight at Kitty Hawk, North Carolina, on December 17, 1903.

5. Airplane Flight—Nonstop by Woman

On July 22, 1933, Amy Johnson Mollison became the first woman to fly nonstop eastward across the Atlantic Ocean. She crashed the second day. She was accompanied on the flight by her husband.

6. Airplane Flight—Solo

The world's first around-the-world solo flight was completed by Wiley H. Post on July 22, 1933, when he landed at Floyd Bennett Field, New York City, after an eastward flight which took him seven days, eighteen hours and forty-five minutes.

7. Airplane Landing on Ship

On January 18, 1911, the first airplane landing was made on the USS Pennsylvania in the harbor at San Francisco, California.

8. Alarm Clock

The first alarm clock was made by Levi Hutchins of Concord, New Hampshire, in 1787. It was twenty-nine inches high and fourteen inches wide and enclosed in a pine case with a mirror on the door. The alarm rang at a fixed time.

9. American Expeditionary Force

On June 30, 1898, the first Expeditionary Force to leave the United States for a destination beyond the Western Hemisphere arrived off Manila, Philippine Islands, led by Admiral George Dewey and General Merritt, in the Spanish-American War. And the first troops of the American Expeditionary Force in World War I reached France on June 26, 1917.

10. Anesthesia

On October 16, 1846, an anesthetic was first used in surgery at the Massachusetts General Hospital.

11. Archbishop of New York

John Hughes became the first archbishop of New York on July 19, 1850. He founded St. John's College.

12. Assassination of President

The first assassination attempt on a United States president occurred on January 30, 1835, when Richard Lawrence, a demented painter, tried to assassinate President Andrew Jackson as he visited the Capitol to attend funeral services for a congressman.

13. Assembly Line Manufacture

Henry Ford revolutionized the manufacture of automobiles by inaugurating his "assembly line" on January 14, 1914, a new technique permitting the assembly of a car while it was in continuous motion.

14. Australian Ballot

On February 24, 1888, Louisville, Kentucky, became the first American city to use the Australian Ballot System.

15. Automatic Telephone

Almon B. Strowger of La Porte, Indiana, inventor, installed the first successful automatic telephone—on November 3, 1892.

16. Automobile

Many think the motor car was invented in the United States. They are wrong. It is to Karl Benz, son of a German engine driver, historians hand the credit. Evidence is that he beat Gottlieb Daimler, the German engineer, to it by about eighteen months. The first Benz car, a three-wheeler, built in Mannheim by the much-ridiculed inventor and his wife, was smacking its solid-tyred lips on the highway in the autumn of 1885. Daimler had been making motor boats, but his first car was not trade-shown until the spring of 1887.

17. Automobile—Ford

Henry Ford drove the first successful Ford around the streets of Detroit in a trial run on June 4, 1896.

18. Automobile—Gas-Propelled

Using the designs of his brother Charles, Frank J. Duryea, a toolmaker, operated the first successful gasoline-propelled motor vehicle made in the United States, on the streets of Springfield, Massachusetts.

19. Automobile License Plates

The Board of examiners of operators of automobiles authorized July 6, 1899, by the City of Chicago, was the first such agency. Its purpose was to ascertain the qualifications of persons seeking licenses. The first automobile license plates were required by the State of New York in 1901. The registration fee was $1 and during the first year the total of fees received was $954. The plates bore the owners' initials and were required to be more than three inches tall.

20. Automobile Race

The first American automobile race was run on a 55-mile course from Chicago to Evanston, Illinois, on November 28, 1895. Of the six cars entered, two were powered by electricity and four by gasoline. It was won by Frank J. Duryea who had an average speed of seven miles per hour. His prize for winning was a $2,000 purse.

21. Automobile Show

The first National Automobile Show opened in Madison Square Gardens, New York City, on November 3, 1900.

22. Balloon Ascent

The space age really began in November, 1783, when man first ascended from the earth in a balloon. Joseph Montgolfier and his brother, Etienne, made a large cloth and paper balloon with an open neck—something like the Fourth of July balloons familiar in the United States before the first World War. They used straw and wool as fuel to fill it with hot smoke. This balloon successfully ascended from Annonay in June of 1783, and when this was reported to the Paris Academy, the brothers were invited to repeat the demonstration in Paris. They built a big seventy-foot balloon, colorfully decorated for the occasion, and it was decided to send two men up in the balloon. François Pilatre de Rozier and Marquis d'Arlandes were chosen from many volunteers, and on the great day the balloon rose from the Bois de Boulogne, stayed aloft almost half an hour and carried the men to the far side of Paris, where it settled safely to the ground.

23. Bank, Savings

The first savings bank was established in New York City on November 29, 1816.

24. Baseball Hall of Fame

On January 29, 1936, the first five men were elected to the Baseball Hall of Fame at Cooperstown, New York. Included were Ty Cobb, Walter Johnson, Christy Mathewson, Honus Wagner, and Babe Ruth.

25. Bathtub

The first bathtub built in the United States was made in Cincinnati in 1842. Constructed of mahogany, lined with sheet lead, it was exhibited at a Christmas party. The next day the local newspapers denounced it as a "luxurious and undemocratic vanity." Doctors warned that the bathtub would be "a menace to health." The next year, in 1843, Philadelphia undertook by public ordinance to prohibit bathing between November 1 and March 15. Two years later Boston made bathing unlawful except when prescribed by a physician.

26. Bible, The

Just a little more than 500 years ago Johann Gutenberg started work on the first complete edition of the Bible which was to be printed from movable type, which he invented. The job took him five years. In the fifteenth century the Bible was "the best seller," and now in the twentieth century, even though it competes with approximately 7,500 new books each year, it still remains the best seller.

27. Bible Printed in America

The first Bible printed in this country was John Eliot's Indian Bible, in 1663. The Indian language in which it was made is extinct. The next Bible printed here was Saur's, in German, in 1743. The first English Bible printed here was at Boston, in small quarto, in 1752.

28. Bicycle

The *Chicago American*, in its issue dated February 14, 1959, reported the evolution of the bicycle as follows:

There is some evidence the Egyptians had some sort of two-wheeled contrivance that was set in motion by a rider's feet. But for all practical purposes, the beginning of the bicycle can be traced to 1817. In that year a German named Baron von Drais introduced a machine which he named the draisine, after himself. The wheels of the draisine were connected by a wooden bar. The rider rested part of his weight on a wooden arm rest in front and propelled himself by kicking the ground, first with one foot and then with the other. He steered by turning a handle on the front wheel, which was pivoted. Because this machine was quite expensive, it was nicknamed "The Dandy Horse." King George IV of England loved to ride one!

About 1840, a Scotsman named Macmillan took an old dandy horse and put cranks on the axle of the rear wheel. These were connected by driving rods with pedals in front. He went so fast with it that he actually was arrested for "furious driving!"

The name bicycle was first used in 1865. A Frenchman named Lallement attached cranks and pedals to the front wheel of a velocipede much like the dandy horse. These "bicycles" were called "boneshakers," because they had heavy wooden frames and iron tires.

In 1868, light metal wheels with wire spokes and solid rubber tires were introduced.

Soon afterward "The Ordinary," a new type of bicycle, appeared. As this developed, the front wheel, which used to be the same size as the real wheel, grew larger and larger. This meant that one circuit of the pedals attached to its axle would drive the bicycle farther. In some models, the front wheel was 5 feet high or even higher, while the rear wheel was only 12 inches in diameter. The rider sat perched above the huge front wheel, and unless he was very skillful, he often was tossed over the handlebars.

Finally, in about 1885, the modern "safety bicycle" was developed. In this type, the wheels were of equal size, and the rider's seat was slightly forward of the rear wheel. By making the sprocket on the pedals much larger than that on the rear wheel, the wheel could be made to cover as much ground at each turn of the pedals as the dangerous large front wheel.

In time other improvements followed to produce the bicycle we have today.

29. "Blackface" Act

The first "blackface" act on the American stage was presented December 30, 1799, when Johann Graupner blackened his face and sang "The Gay Negro Boy" at the Federal Street Theatre in Boston.

30. Blood Bank

The first blood bank to refrigerate blood for transfusions was established March 15, 1937, by the Cook County Hospital in Chicago.

31. Book Matches

On September 27, 1892, Joshua Pusey of Lima, Pennsylvania, patented the first book matches.

32. Books—Pocket Size

Credit for the first venture in publishing pocket-sized books should be given to Aldus Manutius, a Venetian printer of the High Renaissance, who sold numerous pocket editions of the Greek and Latin classics to a book-hungry Europe.

33. Boxing Telecast

On June 19, 1946, the first telecast of a championship heavyweight prize fight originated in New York. Joe Louis KO'd Billy Conn in the eighth round.

34. Boycott

The first boycott law in the United States was enacted in Alabama on September 26, 1903. By it, it was declared to be a misdemeanor for two or more persons to conspire to prevent persons from carrying on a lawful business.

35. Burglar Alarm System

The first burglar alarm was installed by Edwin Thomas Holmes on February 21, 1858, in Boston. The opening of a door or window released a spring which made a contact with the electrical circuit, setting off a bell. The electric bell had been invented in 1831 by Joseph Henry (1797–1878), who became the first head of the Smithsonian Institution. The first burglar alarm system connected by wire to a central office was installed by the Holmes Burglar Alarm Company in New York City in 1872.

36. Cable Car

The cable car was invented by Andrew S. Halliday, and the first one went up Clay Street hill in San Francisco on August 1, 1873.

37. Census

The first census taken in the United States was in 1790, and the returns showed a population of 3,929,214. The idea of taking a census is very ancient and there is evidence that an extensive one was carried out in Babylon about 2,000 B.C. The children of Israel were numbered at the time of the exodus, and censuses were taken at very early dates in China, Egypt, and Prussia. The first modern census dates back to the seventeenth century, the first being held in Quebec and Nova Scotia.

38. Child Born of English Parents in America

Virginia Dare, who was born at Roanoke, Va., on the 18th of August 1587, was the first child born of English parents in America. Her mother, Eleanor Dare, was the daughter of John White, the governor of the colony.

39. Child Born of English Parents in New England

Peregrine White, son of William White and of his wife Susanna, was the first child born of English parents in New England. He was born on board the *Mayflower* in the harbor off Cape Cod on November 20, 1620, and died at Marshfield in 1704.

40. Child Labor Law

On March 28, 1848, the first Child Labor Law was enacted by the State of Pennsylvania, prohibiting children under twelve from engaging in commercial labor, and on September 1, 1917, the first federal Child Labor Law became effective.

41. Christmas Cards

Though the ancient Chinese exchanged New Year cards, the first known modern Christmas card wasn't sent until 1843. Sir Henry Cole, an imaginative and distinguished London museum director, had his artist friend, J. C. Horsley, design 1,000 cards for him which bore the now standard greeting: "A Merry Christmas and a Happy New Year."

42. Christmas Tree—Electrically Lighted

The first Christmas tree lighted by electricity was put in the New York residence of Edward H. Johnson in 1882. This tree had eighty red, white and blue lights on it and was revolved by an electric motor which made the lights blink on and off.

43. Circulating Library

The first circulating library in the United States was established in Philadelphia on November 8, 1731.

44. Circumnavigator of Globe

Ferdinand Magellan, though he did not survive to return home with his ship, well deserves the title of the first world circumnavigator. He discovered the strait which now bears his name, October 20, 1520, the day dedicated in the Catholic calendar to St. Ursula and her eleven thousand virgins, hence he called it "The Strait of the Eleven Thousand Virgins." The strait was passed November 28, and though he had not quite reached the Spice Islands when he fell in conflict with the people of the isle of Matan, April 27, 1521, his task was virtually accomplished, as he had before been as far east as the Spice Islands. The expedition, reduced from five ships and 236 men to one vessel and eighteen men, reached San Lucar, Spain, September 6, 1522, after an absence of three years lacking fourteen days, under the guidance of Juan Sebastian del Cano. This vessel, the Vitoria, was the first to make the circuit of the globe. As a reward Cano was ennobled with the globe on his coat of arms and the motto *Primus circumdedisti me.*

45. Circus—American

The first American circus was established by John Bill Ricketts in 1792 in a building erected especially for his use at 12th and Market streets, Philadelphia. President George Washington attended Ricketts' circus April 22, 1793. Ricketts built a larger structure, called the Art Pantheon and Amphitheatre, which opened to the public in 1795. In 1797, he built an amphitheatre on Greenwich street in New York City and also exhibited in towns as far north as Albany.

46. Clock

Invention of the first clock is credited to Pope Silvester II, 996 A.D., but it probably was more of a curiosity than a dependable working model.

47. Coeducation

On September 6, 1837, women students at Oberlin Collegiate Institute were granted equal academic status with men, making it the first coeducational institution in the United States.

48. Coffee—South American

The first coffee plant, granddaddy of the billions of coffee trees in Latin America which now yield 75 percent of the world's total production, was smuggled to the Western Hemisphere in 1723 by a French naval officer named Gabriel Mathieu Desclieux, stationed on the island of Martinique. Desclieux had petitioned Louis XV for a seedling from a coffee plant which the burgomaster of Amsterdam had sent to Louis XIV's gardener. When the King refused the request, Desclieux and a band of friends sneaked into the royal greenhouse one night and stole a coffee tree.

49. Coffee Break

The white-collar coffee break became official in 1950 when a large New York insurance company called in a restaurant chain to "do something" about the daily chaos caused by 1,700 employees on thirteen floors rushing helter-skelter to and from nearby coffee counters. The restaurant started a catering service, with waitresses rolling carts from typewriter to stenciling machine, and now grosses more than four million dollars a year by doling out thirty million cups of coffee.

50. College Baseball

The first college baseball game was played between Williams and Amherst in 1859. This was not the game originated by Abner Doubleday. It was a form called "Massachusetts ball" and played by rather widely different rules from Doubleday's.

51. College Fraternity

The students at Union College in Schenectady, New York, organized the first college social fraternity, Kappa Alpha, on November 26, 1825.

52. Commandos

First organized and trained in the British Army during World War II, commandos were not new. Fifty years ago the National Guard of the United States had several companies trained to work just like our Commandos. The Marion Zouaves were the first. The company consisted of forty picked men, all between 5 feet 9 inches and 6 feet in height. They were trained for two years in a scientific drill which provided startling results. One of their feats was to scale a wall of smooth boards thirteen feet in height. A squad of cyclists had to scale the same wall carrying their bicycles and rifles with them.

53. Compulsory Automobile Insurance

Massachusetts adopted the first state compulsory insurance act in 1927.

54. Compulsory Military Service—Peacetime

The first peacetime compulsory military service in the United States was inaugurated October 29, 1940, when Secretary of War Henry L. Stimson drew No. 158 from a bowl in the War Department Auditorium in Washington.

55. Compulsory School Attendance Law

On May 18, 1852, Massachusetts became the first state to pass a compulsory education law.

56. Congress, U.S.

Congress met for the first time in Washington on November 17, 1800. It was not until November 21, however, that President John Adams was notified that the Senate at last had a quorum, and on the 22nd he went to the Senate chamber of the new Capitol and addressed Congress, congratulating the members "on the prospect of a residence not to be changed."

57. Conscription

It is a popular belief that conscription for military service was first introduced in 1916 during World War I. This is incorrect. Conscription was introduced into England in 1757 for completing the county quotas of men raised by the Lords Lieutenant. It is true that enrollment was by lot and that substitution was allowed. The Assize of Arms of Henry II in 1181, and the Statute of Winchester in 1285, involved compulsory registration for military service. The array of the Nation, under Queen Elizabeth I, before the war with Spain broke out, also was a compulsory register. In 1916 the Military Service Act (U.S.) was passed after the 1914 attempt to make a voluntary register had failed.

58. Cookbook

The first cookbook published in America was *The Compleat Housewife: or Accomplished Gentlewoman's Companion.* It was modeled after one printed in England. It was published in 1742 at Williamsburg, Virginia, by William Parks. The first cookbook of American authorship was *American Cookery* . . . by Amelia Simmons, printed by Hudson and Goodwin at Hartford, Connecticut, in 1796.

59. Correspondence School

The International Correspondence School, the first institution of its kind, was established at Scranton, Pennsylvania, on October 16, 1891.

60. Cotton Mill—American

Samuel Slater, English expert in textile machinery, started the first American cotton mill on December 20, 1790 at Pawtucket, Rhode Island.

61. Cremation

The first legal cremation in England took place in Woking, the oldest crematorium in the country, in March 1885. Cremation seems to have been practiced in Britain in ancient times as excavations made some years ago near Bridgend, Glamorganshire, brought to light two cairns, both of which were unmistakably of the Bronze Age. One cairn contained the cremated remains of five persons dating from about 1,600 B.C.

62. Crossword Puzzle

The first crossword puzzle was put together by Arthur Winn and appeared in the supplement of the *New York* (Sunday) *World*, December 21, 1913. The first crossword puzzle book was issued April 10, 1924.

63. Dark Horse Presidential Candidate

On May 29, 1844, James K. Polk of Tennessee became the first dark horse candidate in United States political history to receive the presidential nomination as the Democrats ended their national convention at Baltimore.

64. Daylight Saving Time

On March 31, 1918, daylight saving time went into effect throughout the United States for the first time. It lasted only two years. The violent protests of farmers, who said their cows were giving milk an hour after the milk trains passed by, brought repeal of the law over President Wilson's veto. Daylight saving time did not return to the nation as a whole until World War II.

65. Department Store

The first department store was launched by Alexander T. Stewart, on Broadway in New York City. It subsequently was sold to John Wanamaker.

66. Diesel Engine

The first diesel engine built in the United States was made in 1898. The principle of this engine was patented in Germany by Rudolph Diesel in 1892.

67. Direct Primary Election

On May 23, 1903, Wisconsin became the first state to adopt a direct primary for party elections.

68. Dirigible Flight

On July 3, 1878, the first dirigible flight was made by John Wise of Lancaster, Pennsylvania, in a cigar-shaped airship.

69. Duel in U.S.

The first duel in the United States was at Plymouth, Massachusetts, on June 18, 1621, between Edward Doty and Edward Leicester, two servants, both of whom were wounded. For this outrage they were sentenced to the punishment of having their heads and feet tied together, and of lying thus twenty-four hours without food or drink. After suffering, however, in that posture an hour, at their master's intercession and their humble request, with the promise of amendment, they were released by the governor.

70. Earthquake

On August 31, 1886, the first recorded major earthquake to hit the United States jolted Charleston, South Carolina.

71. Electric Fire Alarm

The first electric fire alarm was patented in Boston on May 19, 1857.

72. Electric Locomotive

The first electric locomotive was tested at Washington, D.C. on April 29, 1851.

73. Electric Meter

On August 14, 1888, Oliver B. Shallenberger of Rochester, Pennsylvania, obtained a patent for the first electric meter.

74. Electric Street Railway

Baltimore began the operation of the first electric street railway in the United States in 1885.

75. Electric Washing Machine

The first completely electric washing machine was patented on August 9, 1910.

76. Electro-Magnetic Telegraph

Samuel Finley Breese Morse, a noted American artist, invented the first successful electro-magnetic telegraph. Morse sent the first public telegram "What hath God wrought!" on May 24, 1844, over a forty-mile wire between Washington and Baltimore.

77. Elevated Railroad

The first elevated railroad in the world was opened for traffic in New York City in 1867. It was supported on single columns in Greenwich Street, and its maximum speed was twelve miles per hour. The line was unsuccessful largely because people were afraid to ride it, and it soon went into bankruptcy and was sold at a sheriff's sale.

78. English Book

Sir John Mandeville wrote the first English book in 1356, and in it he showed a correct idea of the form of the earth and of positions in latitude ascertained by observation of the North Pole Star. He knew that there are antipodes and that if ships were sent on voyages of discovery they might sail around the world.

79. Envelopes

Envelopes were rare in the United States in the early 1800's. The first stationer of record to produce handmade envelopes was one Pierson, who manufactured them in New York City from 1839 to 1843. He was succeeded in his business by Jacob Berlin and his son, Harry C. Berlin. In 1847 the latter introduced the first machine for the manufacture of envelopes. The first stamped envelopes issued by the post office appeared in June, 1853. And on February 8, 1898, a patent was issued to J. A. Sherman for the first envelope folding and gumming machine.

80. Father's Day

This day was celebrated for the first time in Spokane, Washington, on June 10, 1919. It was suggested by Mrs. John Bruce Dodd of that city, inspired by her father who had reared a family of six children after the death of their mother.

81. Female Medical Student

Elizabeth Blackwell, who entered the Medical Institution at Geneva, New York, on October 20, 1847, was the first female medical student in the United States.

82. Ferris Wheel

The ferris wheel was first seen at the Columbian Exposition held in Chicago in 1893, the "World's Fair," and was the greatest attraction of all the amusements then offered. It rotated between two pyramids and had a framework of steel 250 feet in diameter and carried 36 cars, each capable of holding 4 passengers. It was designed by and named for George Washington Gale Ferris (1859–96), an engineer of Galesburg, Illinois.

83. Fingerprinting

The two pioneers in introducing the fingerprint system were Sir Francis Gayton (1822–1911) and Sir William Herschel (1833–1917). The latter introduced the system into the Bengal law courts, and then Sir Edward Henry introduced it into the Bengal police service. Sir Edward Henry systemized and codified the fingerprint system in his famous work, *Classification and Uses of Fingerprints,* and it was he who founded the Fingerprint Bureau at New Scotland Yard in 1901.

84. Fire Department

The first paid fire department in the United States was established in Boston in 1679. Boston ordered a hand-operated fire engine from England and employed thirteen men to operate it. The first volunteer fire department was founded in Philadelphia in 1736 by Benjamin Franklin. The first salaried, steam-operated fire department was established in Cincinnati in 1853.

85. First Lady of the Land

Lucy Ware Webb Hayes, the wife of our nineteenth president, Rutherford B. Hayes, was called "the first lady of the land" in an account of the inauguration of President Hayes on March 4, 1877, written by Mary Clemner, one of the most talented women reporters of her time. This reference to the President's wife did not attain wide journalistic use, however, until after the production in 1911–12 of Charles Nerdinger's play about President James Madison's wife Dolly, "The First Lady of the Land."

86. Floating Hospital

The world's first floating hospital, the *Emma Abbot,* was launched at New York City on July 19, 1875.

87. Football

The first football game in the United States was played at Mansfield, Pennsylvania, on September 29, 1892.

88. Fork

Although gold and silver forks were made in the thirteenth century, the fork did not become a table implement in England until the seventeenth century. Queen Elizabeth was the first English sovereign to use a fork at the table.

89. Gas Lighting

It was on February 17, 1817, that an American city was first illuminated by gas light. The city was Baltimore, Maryland.

90. Gasoline Tax

On February 25, 1919, Oregon became the first state to tax gasoline. The rate was one percent of the cost of the gasoline and the funds went to the state.

91. Gold Discovered in California

The discovery of gold in California on August 19, 1848 was first reported in the *New York Herald*.

92. Government Bank

The first government incorporated bank in the United States was the Bank of North America, chartered by the Continental Congress in 1781. It began operations in Philadelphia on January 7, 1782, and it supplied aid to the government in the closing months of the American Revolution. Among its original depositors and stockholders were Thomas Jefferson, Alexander Hamilton, John Paul Jones, Benjamin Franklin, James Monroe, and John Jay.

93. Grand Opera

On October 7, 1600, grand opera was introduced to the world in Florence, Italy, by a performance of *Eurydice*, at the wedding of Henry IV of France to an Italian princess. The first nationwide broadcast in the United States of a complete opera took place in 1931, when *Hansel and Gretel* was presented direct from the Metropolitan Opera House in New York.

94. Group Insurance

On July 1, 1912, the first large group insurance was written on employees of Montgomery Ward & Company of Chicago.

95. Guillotine

The guillotine was first officially used in Paris on April 25, 1792. Contrary to popular belief, the device wasn't invented by Dr. Joseph I. Guillotin. He merely recommended to the constituent assembly the use of a mechanized knife.

96. Gunpowder

The first general to use gunpowder in warfare was Genghis Khan, who conquered China in 1215.

97. Gymnasium

The first American gymnasium was opened on September 26, 1825, at Roundhill School, Northampton, Massachusetts. It was founded by Carl Beck from Germany and marked the beginning in the United States of the German Turnverein movement.

98. Holly

Holly was first used in English windows to indicate Christian worship, as the red berries were supposed to represent the blood of Jesus. The holly was believed to keep evil spirits away.

99. Homestead Act

On January 1, 1863, the Homestead Act of the United States went into effect. The first homesteader was Daniel Freeman, a soldier in the Northern Army, who staked out a claim near Beatrice, Nebraska.

100. Hospital in U.S.

On January 4, 1751, the first hospital in the United States was founded at Philadelphia, Pennsylvania. It was known as Pennsylvania Hospital.

101. Hybrid Seed Corn

The first shipment of hybrid seed corn was made on April 13, 1916 from Jacobsburg, Ohio.

102. Hydrogen Bomb

The first United States hydrogen-device explosion took place in the Pacific Ocean on November 1, 1952.

103. Ice Cream Freezer

On May 30, 1848, the first ice cream freezer was patented by William G. Young of Baltimore, Maryland.

104. Incandescent Lamp

The incandescent lamp was invented by Thomas A. Edison on October 21, 1879.

105. Income Tax

The first income tax, in the modern sense, was imposed in England by William Pitt in 1799 to help pay for the wars with Napoleon. It was abolished after the peace of Amiens in 1802. The following year when war again broke out with France, the tax was reimposed. After Waterloo it was abolished once more. Then in 1842 the British government adopted the income tax as a permanent feature in its revenue system.

In 1861 the United States government levied a tax on income for the first time in history. All income in excess of $800 was taxed at a 3 percent rate.

106. Indian Reservation

The first Indian reservation was established by the New Jersey legislature at Indian Mills, on August 29, 1758.

107. Intercollegiate Baseball

The first intercollegiate baseball game was played between Amherst and Williams at Pittsfield, Massachusetts, on July 1, 1859.

108. International Airport

On October 28, 1927, the first international air passenger station in the United States was opened at Key West, Florida.

109. Iron Lung

On October 12, 1928, the iron lung (respirator) was first used at Children's Hospital, Boston, Massachusetts, on a little girl suffering from infantile paralysis.

110. Jet Plane Flight

Robert Stanley made the first American jet plane flight on October 1, 1942.

111. Jewish Sunday School

On March 4, 1838, the first Jewish Sunday school was organized by Rebecca Gratz at Philadelphia, Pennsylvania.

112. Kennedy, John F.

President John F. Kennedy possessed a whole series of "firsts" in relation to his November 8, 1960 election. He was the first Catholic elected president; he was the first Navy veteran; he was the youngest, at 43, ever accorded a victory vote for the top elective honor; and he was the only presidential elective accorded such rank during the lifetime of a grandparent, his maternal grandmother.

113. Kindergarten

Samuel L. Hill opened the first private kindergarten for free instruction on January 3, 1876, in Florence, Massachusetts.

114. Labor Day Parade

On September 5, 1882, the first Labor Day parade was held in New York City.

115. Labor Strike

The first strike on record was in Rome in 309 B.C. when a Greek flute player named Aristos called his orchestra out because they weren't allowed to eat lunch in the temple where they performed.

116. Labor Unions

New Jersey was the first state to legalize a labor union, on February 14, 1883.

117. League of Nations

The first meeting of the Assembly of the League of Nations took place at Geneva, Switzerland, on November 14, 1920. Delegates of forty-one nations were present. The United States was the only major world power absent.

118. Life Insurance

The first non-forfeitable life insurance policy was written by the New York Life Insurance Company on August 13, 1860.

119. Locomotive

On September 27, 1825, in England, George Stephenson operated the first locomotive to haul a passenger train. It carried thirty-four passengers at fifteen miles per hour.

The first locomotive manufactured in the United States was completed at West Point Foundry in 1830, and on January 15, 1831, "The Best Friend of Charleston," the first practical American-built locomotive, made its first run over the Charleston and Hamburg Railroad in South Carolina.

120. Long Distance Telephone

On October 18, 1892, the first commercial long distance telephone line was opened between New York and Chicago.

121. Magazine

On February 13, 1741, Andrew Bradford of Philadelphia published the first magazine in the United States. It was called *The American Magazine* or a Monthly Review of the Political State of the British

Colonies. And on February 7, 1818, the first educational magazine in America to achieve success, the *Academician,* was published in New York.

122.   Mariner's Compass

The compass as a guide to sailors was used by the Chinese as far back as 2364 B.C. But its first *recorded* use in sea travel was made by a Chinese writer in about 750 B.C. It was brought to Europe by Marco Polo.

123.   Marriage—Medical Tests

On April 12, 1938, New York became the first state to require medical tests for marriage license applicants.

124.   Medicine, Practice of

On September 26, 1772, New Jersey became the first state to pass a law regulating the practice of medicine.

125.   Memorial Day

On May 30, 1868, the first formal observance of Memorial Day took place following the request of General John A. Logan, Commander in Chief of the Grand Army of the Republic.

126.   Mid-Air Refueling

On June 27, 1923, the first refueling in mid air was made by Air Corps Captain Lowell Smith and Air Corps Lieutenant John Richter from a forty-foot steel-wire-encased hose lowered to the fuel-receiving plane.

127.   Motion Pictures

The first public showing of a motion picture was held April 23, 1896, at the old Koster and Beale Music Hall in New York City. And on December 3, 1922, the first successful Technicolor motion picture, "The Toll of the Sea," was shown at the Rialto Theatre in that city.

128. Motion Picture Camera

On August 31, 1887, Thomas A. Edison patented the kinescope, the first moving picture camera.

129. Motion Picture Censorship

The State of Pennsylvania set up the first moving picture censorship board on June 19, 1911.

130. Museum

The first public museum in America was the Charleston Museum, South Carolina. It was organized January 12, 1773. The first curators were Charles Cotesworthy Pinckney, Thomas Heyward, Alexander Baron, and Peter Fayssoux. Pinckney later was a member of the convention that drafted the Constitution (1787); Heyward was a signer of the Declaration of Independence; and Fayssoux was a physician in the Revolutionary Army.

131. National Banking System

On February 25, 1863, the first United States National Banking System was created by act of Congress, and on June 20, 1863, the National Bank of Davenport, Iowa, was the first national bank to be chartered under the new banking law.

132. Naval Post Office

On August 20, 1908, the first post office aboard a naval vessel was established on the USS Nebraska.

133. Negro University

Howard University, Washington, D.C., the first Negro university to establish undergraduate, graduate and professional schools, was founded on November 20, 1866.

134. Neutrality, U.S.

On April 27, 1793, President George Washington issued our first neutrality proclamation, in a war between Great Britain and France.

135. Newspaper

The first newspaper on record was *The Peking News*, which began publication 950 years before the invention of printing from movable type. It went out of existence only so recently as 1935, at the ripe old age of 1,572 years.

The first English publication that had any similarity to the modern newspaper was *Nathaniel Butter's Weekly News* (1622). The *London Gazette*, begun in 1665, is still being published. The first daily newspaper in England was the *Daily Courant*, begun in 1702.

The first American news sheet was issued in Boston in 1690. This publication, *Publick Occurrences*, was suppressed by royal authority after only one issue. The first American daily newspaper was the *Pennsylvania Packet and Daily Advertiser*, which appeared in Philadelphia in 1784 and existed as such until 1839.

As a matter of indisputable historical fact, the oldest U.S. daily is the *New York Post*, which has been in continuous daily publication since 1801. And as for the country's oldest newspaper, daily or weekly, that title, too, lies beyond doubt. In 1837, a 73-year-old Hartford weekly named the *Connecticut Courant* put forth a daily edition called the *Hartford Courant*. Thus the U.S.'s oldest newspaper describes an ancestorless continuum that is a straight line two centuries long.

136. Newspaper Cartoon

The first newspaper cartoon in America appeared on May 9, 1754, when Benjamin Franklin's "Join or Die" cartoon was printed in the *Pennsylvania Gazette*. It depicted a dissected snake, each part labeled with the name of a colony.

137. New York Stock Exchange

This exchange was started when twenty-four New York brokers met under a buttonwood tree on May 17, 1792, on the present site of 68 Wall Street and agreed to fix uniform rates of commission on the sale of stocks and bonds.

138. Niagara Falls

On March 29, 1848, for the first time in recorded history Niagara Falls stopped flowing.

139. Nobel Prizes

The Nobel prizes were distributed for the first time on December 10, 1910.

140. Novel

The first novel written in America by an American was *The Power of Sympathy; or, The Triumph of Nature,* attributed to Sarah Wentworth Morton, but now believed to have been written by her neighbor, William Hill Brown. It was printed by the great pioneer printer, Isaiah Thomas, in Boston in 1789.

141. Nuclear Chain Reaction

On December 2, 1942, a self-sustaining nuclear chain reaction was demonstrated for the first time by a group of scientists working in great secrecy below the football stadium at the University of Chicago.

142. One-Way Traffic

On December 17, 1791, New York City established the first one-way traffic regulation in the United States.

143. Opera in the U.S.

On November 29, 1825, the first grand opera, the *Barber of Seville,* was sung at the Park Theatre in New York City.

144. Parachute Jump

There is evidence that Chinese acrobats used parachute-like devices as early at 1306. Although Leonardo da Vinci was the first person to study parachutes from the point of view of aeronautics, it was not until

1783 that the first parachute was invented by Sebastian Lenormand, and his intention was that it should be used as a fire-escaping device.

The modern parachute is regarded as the invention of Francois Blanchard who in 1785 dropped a dog from a balloon, successfully using the parachute. The first human descent by parachute was made by Andre-Jacques Garnerin, who made five jumps from a balloon between 1797 and 1804, the last from an altitude of 8,000 feet. Captain Albert Berry performed the first parachute jump from an airplane on March 12, 1912, when he jumped at Jefferson Barracks, Missouri.

145.   Parasite

Among early Greeks, one who provided entertainment at tables of the rich, especially flattery, was called a *parasitos* (para, beside; *sitos,* food). The term became *parasitus* in Latin.

146.   Patentee

The first patent granted by the United States government was issued to Samuel Hopkins of Vermont on July 31, 1790. The document, signed by President George Washington, Secretary of State Thomas Jefferson, and Attorney General Edmund Randolph, was for a "process of making potash and pearl ashes." Only three patents were issued that year.

147.   Pencil

Graphite, from which so-called lead pencils are made, was discovered in Cumberland, England, in 1564. It is not lead at all but gets its name from the leaden color of writing done with it. The first wooden pencil was invented around 1686 in France. Before that advance, graphite was pushed into quills or tubes, wound with string, or put into metal holders called *port-carons*. It takes about 2.8 board feet of wood to make twelve dozen pencils.

148.   Penitentiary

The first institution of this kind in the United States is said to have been established in 1786 by the Quakers. The principal objects of a penitentiary should be, says Blackstone, "to preserve and amend the health of the unhappy offenders, to enure them to habits of industry, to guard them from pernicious company."

149. Petroleum

First discovery of the great petroleum resources of the United States came about during the boring of salt wells. In some wells, petroleum or "rock oil" was present. First the oil was used as medicine, then to light homes. In 1859, Pennsylvania's rich source of supply was discovered and Civil War veterans rushed to the fields. Now about one and one-half billion barrels annually come from America's oil fields.

150. Platinum

Platinum was first discovered in the Choco district of Colombia. It was regarded by the Spaniards as worse than worthless and in the beginning it was thrown away. In 1824 Mallieu reports that its selling price at this locality was twelve to sixteen shillings a pound. Its present value is well over a hundred dollars an ounce.

151. Plywood

The first commercial factories to make plywood were erected in Russia in the 1880's.

152. Poet Laureate

On August 9, 1631, John Dryden, the English poet, dramatist, and satirist was appointed the first poet laureate of England.

153. Polio Vaccine

It was on February 23, 1954, that Salk anti-poliomyelitis vaccine was first used in a mass innoculation of school children, at Pittsburgh, Pennsylvania.

154. Political Convention

The first national political convention was held in Baltimore, Maryland, on September 26, 1831. The Anti-Masonic Party nominated William Wirt of Maryland for the presidency.

155. Postage Stamps—U.S.

The first postage stamps in this country were issued in accordance with an act of Congress approved March 3, 1847. They were of five- and ten-cent denominations, and the date of issue was designated as July 1.

156. Postal Service

On January 22, 1773, the first regular postal route was established from Boston to New York City. A round trip was made each month.

157. Presidential Nominating Conventions

The first presidential nominating conventions were held in 1832— both the Democratic and the National Republican (later Whig)—in Baltimore. Since then Chicago has been host of fourteen Republican conventions and nine Democratic conventions. The Progressive (Bull Moose) convention of 1912 also was held in Chicago, making a total of twenty-four conventions held in that city. Baltimore has been the second most popular choice, with thirteen conventions.

158. Presidential Succession

On April 6, 1841, exactly one month after his election, President William Henry Harrison died of pneumonia in the White House. John Tyler, Vice President, succeeded him as the tenth president of the United States and the first to assume the presidency by virtue of the death of a president.

159. Printing

A South African professor has deciphered writings on a disk, known as the Phalstos Disk, which was found in the palace of Phalstos, Southern Crete, in 1908. All previous attempts to decipher the writing or to determine the language in which it is written have failed but it is now believed to be the earliest example of printing in the world and may well be more than 3,500 years old.

160. Public Library

On April 9, 18£3, the townspeople of Petersborough, New Hampshire, founded the first public library in the nation to be supported by municipal taxes.

161. Radar

On September 27, 1922, the first radar observations were made at Anacostia, D.C. It was first used to detect enemy airplanes at Pearl Harbor on December 7, 1941.

162. Radio Broadcast

On May 12, 1908, the first radio broadcast demonstration took place and on that day a patent was issued to Nathan B. Stubblefield to transmit a voice by air without the aid of wires. It was on June 14, 1922, that Warren G. Harding became the first president of the United States to speak over the radio.

163. Radio Broadcasting Station

The first commercial radio station in the United States was 8MK (now WWJ), Detroit. This station began daily service August 20, 1920, with the program "Tonight's Dinner." The station first broadcast local election returns August 31, 1920. KDKA, Pittsburgh, began regular broadcasts Novembu. 2, 1920, with the Harding-Cox presidential election returns.

164. Radio Comedians

The first real comedians of radio broadcasting, Billy Jones and Ernie Hare, went on the air for the Happiness Candy Company, and were billed as "The Happiness Boys."

165. Refrigerator

On October 2, 1860, a United States patent was granted for an ice-making machine, the forerunner of the modern refrigerator.

166. Religious Service Broadcast

On January 2, 1921, religious services were broadcast for the first time by Station KDKA, Pittsburgh, Pennsylvania.

167. Revolution, Blood Shed in

The first blood shed in the American Revolution was in the conflict known as the "Boston Massacre," between the British soldiers and the citizens of Boston, March 5, 1770.

168. Rose Bowl Football

It was on January 1, 1902, that the first Rose Bowl football match took place at Pasadena, California.

169. Safety Razor

An eighteenth century Parisian named Jean Jacques Perrett became tired of having his face cut while his barber shaved him. Wouldn't shaving be much safer and more comfortable, he wondered, if a wooden guard were attached to the straight razor blade so that only a snip of the blade protruded? And so was born the safety razor.

170. Sales Tax—State

When West Virginia, on May 3, 1921, imposed a state sales tax, it became the first state to do so.

171. Satellite

On October 4, 1957, Soviet scientists launched Sputnik I, first man-made satellite, which circled the earth every one-and-a-half hours.

172. Savings Bank

The first savings bank in the United States was founded in Philadelphia, Pennsylvania, by the Philadelphia Savings Fund Society on February 25, 1819.

173. Scientific Society—National

The first national scientific society organization, the American Association for the Advancement of Science, was organized on September 20, 1848, at Philadelphia, Pennsylvania.

174. Self-Service Restaurant

On September 4, 1885, the Exchange Buffet in New York City was the first self-service restaurant opened in the United States.

175. Self-Winding Clock

A patent for the first self-winding clock was applied for on October 6, 1783, by B. Hanks of Litchfield, Connecticut.

176. Ship—Electrically Propelled

On April 7, 1913, the first electrically propelled ship of the United States Navy, USS Jupiter, was commissioned.

177. Shoe Manufacturing Machine

On July 6, 1858, Lyman Reed Blake of Abington, Massachusetts, received a patent for the first shoe manufacturing machine.

178. Shorthand

Although many are under the impression that shorthand is a modern invention, systems of shorthand have been in use for many centuries. Julius Caesar is said to have used shorthand and the Emperor Titus used to boast that he could take down speeches more quickly than even the professional shorthand writers. The most widely used systems today are Gregg and Pitman. Sir Isaac Pitman, who was born in 1813, published his *Stenographic Sound-Hand* in 1837.

179. Sidewalks of New York

The sidewalks of New York, famous in song and story, were started by a woman, the Widow Provoost. She was only twenty-six years old when her husband died in 1820, but she immediately took charge of his importing business. This establishment was away from the main thoroughfare, and in bad weather the mud was deep enough to discourage even the most hardy of patrons. In order to make her store more accessible she ordered a large number of flat stones laid as a sidewalk from the thoroughfare past her place and on to the next street. Curiosity brought people to see and try out the new sidewalk and of course they stopped in the store and bought many things they needed.

180. Skyscraper

The first building known as a skyscraper was a ten-story structure erected by the Home Insurance Company of New York at the northeast corner of La Salle and Adams streets in Chicago. It was designed by Major William Le Baron Jenney and built in 1884-5. It was constructed of marble, flanked by four columns of polished granite supporting a marble balcony. Two stories were added later. A steel frame supported the entire weight of the walls.

181. Sleeping Cars

The first sleeping cars ever designed were built in 1838 and used on the Cumberland Valley Railroad between Harrisburg and Chambersburg, Pennsylvania.

182. Small Claims Court

On March 15, 1913, the first conciliation tribunal for small claims was established as the Conciliation Branch of the Municipal Court of Cleveland, Ohio. The plaintiff could not be represented by counsel but was required to present his own case.

183. Smallpox Vaccination

On June 26, 1721, the first innoculations against smallpox were given in America.

184. Soda Water

Soda water was first prepared, shortly after 1800, by Townsend Speakman of Philadelphia, who carbonated water for Dr. Philip Syng Physick, the "father of American surgery." It was dispensed from fountains for patients at $1.50 per month for one glass a day. In 1807 he added fruit juices to make the drink more palatable.

185. Sound Film

On March 13, 1923, Lee De Forest's *Phonofilm,* the first sound-on-film moving picture, was demonstrated. Music, but no voices, was heard.

186. Sports Competition

The first competitive sports event held by white men in America was a lawn bowling tournament. It took place in the Jamestown colony in 1607, at the end of the first summer of the first English-speaking settlement in North America.

187. Steamboat Invention

The first practical success in steam navigation was made by John Fitch, a native of Windsor, Connecticut, who had settled in New Jersey as a silversmith. In August of 1785, he petitioned Congress for aid in constructing a vessel to be propelled by steam, and with the pecuniary assistance of several gentlemen he immediately undertook to build a steamboat which was successfully tested in the fall of 1787. The steamer moved in dead water at the rate of eight miles an hour, or one mile in seven and a half minutes. With thirty passengers the boat left Philadelphia and, moving against the current of the Delaware, reached Burlington, a distance of twenty miles, in three hours and ten minutes.

188. Steamship—Atlantic Crossing

In the year 1819 the first steam vessel crossed the Atlantic. The name of the ship was the *Savannah,* and she made the journey across the ocean largely with the assistance of her sails.

189. Steeplechase

The first steeplechase in turf history was run in Ireland in 1752, over four miles of country between Buttevant and Doneraile (County Cork), the winning post being the steeple of Doneraile Parish Church. Today the prowess of the Irish horse is celebrated the world over. Nashua, bred in County Kildare, won the greatest total of prize money ($1,288,565) in the annals of the American turf, and Irish-bred horses have won forty of the last fifty English Grand Nationals—the most coveted prize in steeplechasing.

190. Stethoscope

In 1816, a French doctor, Rene Laennec, watched boys playing with a wooden plank. As one tapped at one end, another listened at the other. Observing how sound traveled through the plank, Dr. Laennec later rolled paper into a cylinder and placed one end at the patient's chest, the other at his ear. This was the first stethoscope.

191. Streetcar

On November 14, 1832, the first streetcar in the world made its appearance on the streets of New York. New Yorkers referred to the new contrivance as a "horse car." Thirty persons could be accommodated in the three compartments and it operated from City Hall to 14th Street.

192. Street Lighting

Paris was the first city to have street lighting. About the year 1700, each householder was ordered to keep a lamp burning all night in a window nearest the street. A few years later, tallow-burning lanterns suspended over the streets were installed.

193. Subway

On September 1, 1897, the first subway in America, the Boston Municipal, was opened for traffic.

194. Supersonic Flight

On October 14, 1947, Captain Charles Yeager of the U.S. Air Force at Muroc, California, piloted the first supersonic flight—an airplane faster than the speed of sound.

195. Tabloid Newspaper

The first United States tabloid newspaper, the *New York Daily News*, was published June 26, 1919. The founders were Colonel Robert R. McCormick and his cousin, Joseph M. Patterson, also the publishers of the *Chicago Tribune* at that time.

196. Talking Motion Picture

The first motion picture made was a "talkie," although sound pictures did not come into general use until 1927. Thomas A. Edison made the first movie in 1889. It was accompanied by sound synchronized from a phonograph record, another Edison invention.

197. Telegraph

On January 6, 1838, Samuel F. B. Morse and Arthur Vail demonstrated the telegraph publicly for the first time at Speedwell Ironworks, Morristown, New Jersey, and on October 18, 1842, Morse laid the first telegraph cable in New York Harbor between the Battery and Governor's Island.

198. Telegraph Patent

The first patent for a telegraph in the United States was received by Jonathan Grout, Jr. of Belchertown, Massachusetts, on October 24, 1800. It was a signaling system operated from hilltop to hilltop between Martha's Vineyard and Boston, sighted by telescope.

199. Telephone Conversation

The first telephone conversation over out-of-door wires was conducted October 9, 1876, between Boston and Cambridge, Massachusetts.

200. Telephone Directory

On February 21, 1878, the first telephone directory was issued by the New Haven (Conn.) Telephone Company. It listed fifty subscribers and was the first of its kind in the world.

201. Telephone Switchboard

On May 17, 1877, Edwin T. Holmes, operator of the Holmes Burglar Alarm Service, installed the first telephone switchboard in his Boston office and it served as a telephone service by day and a burglar alarm by night.

202. Television

On May 11, 1928, station WGY, Schenectady, New York, began the first regularly scheduled television programs. The first outdoor television scenes were viewed on July 12, 1928, by the Bell Telephone Laboratories in New York City.

203. Thanksgiving Day

On November 28, 1863, the nation observed the first Thanksgiving Day set aside by national proclamation.

204. Thermometer

Galileo Galilei (1564–1642) constructed one of the first thermometers. It consisted of a small glass bulb to which was attached a tube immersed in a colored liquid. Changes in temperature in the bulb caused the height of the liquid in the tube to vary. Later the liquid was changed to alcohol.

In 1701, Sir Isaac Newton devised a method of calibrating the alcohol thermometer, establishing a range between the freezing state of water and the temperature of the human body.

Gabriel Daniel Fahrenheit (1686–1736) introduced the Fahrenheit scale. He used as a base for his lowest temperature a condition caused by mixing salt and ice. The interval on the scale between the lowest temperature (zero) and the temperature of the human body was divided into 96 equal parts. The temperature of the body was 96 degrees and that of the freezing point of water was at 32 degrees. After Fahrenheit's death the upper limit was set at 212 degrees, the boiling point of water, and the interval between these points was divided into 180 equal parts, or degrees.

205. Toasts

In *Alexandre Dumas' Dictionary of Cuisine,* published by Simon & Schuster, Inc., New York, we are told that toasts were first drunk in France at the time of the Revolution. The name comes from the English, who when they drank anyone's health, put a piece of toast on the bottom of the beer pot. Whoever drank last got the toast. One day Anne Boleyn, then the most beautiful woman in England, was taking her bath, surrounded by the lords of her suite. These gentlemen, courting her favor, each took a glass, dipped it in the tub, and drank her health. All but one, who was asked why he did not follow the example. "I am waiting for the toast," he said.

206. Tobacco

On November 14, 1492, Christopher Columbus noted in his journal the use of tobacco among the Indians of the New World, the first recorded reference to tobacco.

207. Trademark Registration

The first trademark registration was achieved in 1870.

208. Traffic Laws

On June 27, 1652, New Amsterdam, now New York City, enacted the first traffic law.

209. Train Robbery

The first train robbery was made on October 6, 1866, by the Reno brothers, two of whom, John and Simeon, boarded an Ohio and Mississippi train, clubbed the Adams express agent, and looted a safe containing $15,000. They had to abandon another safe containing $30,000 when a posse arrived on handcars. The gang struck again on May 22, 1868, looting a Jeffersonville, Madison and Indianapolis train. The haul was a whopping $96,000, triple what the James boys ever got in a single robbery. Three of the brothers and six other gang members eventually were captured, but all nine were taken from the authorities and lynched by vigilantes.

210. Transatlantic Air Express

The first transatlantic air express service was inaugurated in 1941.

211. Transatlantic Flights

Amelia Earhart became the first woman to fly across the Atlantic Ocean when she took off from Newfoundland as a passenger in a plane piloted by Wilmer Stultz on June 17, 1928. The first commercial airplane service across the Atlantic was inaugurated on May 9, 1936, and the first round-trip flight was completed by Richard Mitchell and Harry Richman, on September 13, 1936. Pan American Airways started the first regular air passenger service across the Atlantic on May 20, 1939, as the *Yankee Clipper* took off from Port Washington, New York, bound for Europe.

212. Transatlantic Radio Broadcast

On January 19, 1903, the first regular transatlantic broadcast was sent between Cape Cod, Massachusetts, and Cornwall, England. Greetings were exchanged between President Theodore Roosevelt and King Edward VII.

213. Transatlantic Telephone Service

On January 7, 1927, regular transatlantic telephone service was inaugurated between London and New York.

214. Transcontinental Automobile Trip

On August 31, 1903, a Packard automobile ended a fifty-two day journey from San Francisco to New York, the first time an automobile had crossed the continent under its own power.

215. Transcontinental Flight—Woman

On November 24, 1930, for the first time in history a woman aviator, Ruth Nichols, made a transcontinental flight from New York to California. It took her seven days.

216. Transpacific Air Mail

On November 22, 1935, the *China Clipper* left San Francisco for the first official transpacific air mail flight. An 8,000 mile trip, it arrived at Manila after four stops, seven days later.

217. Transpacific Cable

On July 4, 1903, the first Pacific cable from San Francisco to Manila was opened. President Theodore Roosevelt sent a message around the world; it came back to him in twelve minutes.

218. Typewriter

The first United States patent on a typewriter was granted in 1829 to William Austin Burt of Detroit. The only model of this machine was destroyed by fire in 1836. The first real step in the progress of mechanized office equipment was made in 1867, when Christopher Latham Sholes, Wisconsin journalist and grandfather of office machinery, invented the typewriter. His first machine was crude and bulky. Its keyboard was made of black walnut wood with letters and numbers painted white; the type spaced unevenly and often stuck. But crude as it was, it had the basic features of the modern typewriter. On March 1, 1873, the first practical typewriter was manufactured by E. Remington & Sons.

219. Umbrella

Originated in Asiatic countries, the umbrella was introduced from Italy into England in the eighteenth century. Used at first as a protection against the sun's rays, it was shunned by men as effeminate until Jonas Hanway, an English traveler, demonstrated its usefulness as a protection against rain. It is believed to have been first used in the United States in Windsor, Connecticut, in 1740. At first, sight of it caused merriment among townsfolk, and some wags paraded after the user carrying sieves attached to broomsticks.

220. United Nations General Assembly

The first session of the General Assembly of the United Nations convened in London on January 10, 1946.

221. Vacuum Cleaners

The first vacuum cleaner was patented by Ives W. McGuffey on June 8, 1869.

222. Vatican Broadcast

On February 12, 1931, the first broadcast was made from the Vatican by Pope Pius XI. The Vatican radio station HVJ was installed by Marconi, the inventor of wireless telegraphy.

223. Vending Machine

The first vending machine goes back to 219 B.C. when Hero Ostebus, a Grecian high priest, invented a device for dispensing holy water at a drop of a (drachma) coin.

224. Venetian Blinds

The famous world traveler of the thirteenth century, Marco Polo, was the man believed to be responsible for introducing Venetian blinds to the West. It is said he saw them in China and brought the idea back to Venice where they acquired their western name.

225. Voting Machine

On March 15, 1892, New York became the first state to authorize the use of voting machines.

226. War Loans

On December 23, 1776, the United States floated her first loan for war purposes.

227. Watch

Watches were first made at Nuremberg, Germany, in 1477 by Peter Hele. His first watch varied nearly an hour a day from the true time and required winding twice a day. It was egg-shaped and about the size of a goose egg, hence it was sometimes called the "Nuremberg animated egg." The statement made by some that Robert, King of Scotland, had a watch about the year 1310, doubtless is erroneous. The invention of spring watches has been ascribed to Dr. Robert Hooke, and by some to Huygens about 1658; the anchor escapement was invented by Clement in 1680; the horizontal watch by George Graham in 1724; the repeating watch by Barlowe in 1676; and Harrison produced his first timepiece in 1735.

228. Waves

On July 7, 1948, the first women sworn into the United States Navy took the oath of office administered by Rear Admiral George Lucius Russell at Washington, D.C.

229. Weather Observations

The first weather observations in the United States were taken by Josiah Meigs (1757–1822). As commissioner-general of the general land office in 1817, he ordered observations taken three times a day in the land offices.

230. White Child Born in America

The first white child, of which we have any record, was Snorre Thorfinnson, who was born at Straumfjord (Buzzard's Bay), in the present state of Massachusetts, in the year 1008. He was the son of Thorfinn Karlsefne and his wife Gudrid. From him the famous sculptor, Albert Thorwaldsen, is lineally descended, besides a long train of learned and distinguished men who have flourished during the last eight centuries in Iceland and Denmark.

231. Wireless Telegraphy

On July 20, 1910, wireless telegraphy was first used by Scotland Yard to apprehend a criminal. They wired a ship at sea to stop at Quebec where Dr. Crippen, a wife murderer, was caught.

232.   Woman Baseball Player

On April 1, 1931, Virnie Miller, nineteen years old, was the first woman baseball player in history to be signed up. It was as a pitcher and the team was the Chattanooga (Tennessee) Baseball Club.

233.   Woman Cabinet Member

On March 4, 1933, Frances Perkins became the first woman member of the cabinet when she was appointed Secretary of Labor by President Franklin D. Roosevelt.

234.   Woman Hanged in U.S.

Mary Dyer, a Quakeress, was the first woman hanged in the United States. On the gallows for the second time June 1, 1660, she was offered her life if she would promise to stay out of Massachusetts. Her reply was, "In obedience to the will of the Lord I came; and in his will I abide faithful to the death."

235.   Woman in Congress

Jeanette Rankin (R.) of Montana was the first woman elected to the House of Representatives. She was elected to the 65th Congress (March 4, 1917 to March 3, 1919). She did not seek renomination but was an unsuccessful candidate for the Senate. She returned to the House in 1941–1943.

236.   Woman in Senate

On October 3, 1922, Mrs. Rebecca L. Felton, a Georgia Democrat, was the first woman in the United States to be seated in the Senate. She received a temporary appointment from the Governor of Georgia to fill a vacancy caused by the death of Senator Thomas E. Watson. She served until November 22, 1922, when her elected successor took his seat in the Senate.

237. Woman Pharmacist

On March 16, 1883, Susan Hayhurst became the first woman pharmacist upon her graduation from the Philadelphia College of Pharmacy with the degree of Ph.C.

238. Woman Physician

The first woman physician of modern times was Dr. Elizabeth Blackwell (1821–1910), a native of England who came to the United States as a girl and received the M.D. degree in 1849 at the Geneva Medical School of western New York.

239. Woman Suffrage

Wyoming was admitted in 1890 as the 44th state of the United States. Its constitution called for woman suffrage—the first state to grant this.

240. Woman Telegrapher

On February 21, 1846, Sarah Bagley became the first woman telegrapher in history—at Lowell, Massachusetts, in the office of the New York and Boston Magnetic Telegraph Company.

241. World's Fair

The first great world exposition and trade fair was held in Hyde Park, London, in 1851. It covered twenty-one acres, had 13,937 exhibitors and drew an attendance of more than six million persons. The main building of this fair was the nucleus of the building later known as the Crystal Palace.

242. Zoological Garden

Zoo is short for zoological garden, and is a place where living animals are kept and exhibited. The first zoo we know anything about was called an "intelligence park." It was started as long ago as 1150 B.C. by

ZOOLOGICAL GARDEN

a Chinese emperor, and it had many kinds of deer, birds, and fish in it.

The first real public zoological garden in the world was opened in Paris in 1793. This was the famous *Jardin des Plantes,* and in it were animals, a museum and a botanical garden.

The next big zoological garden to be opened was in 1829 in Regent's Park in London. Then came the Zoological Garden of Berlin, which was begun in 1844 and became one of the finest and best in the world.

In the United States, the first zoo to be opened was in Philadelphia in 1874, and the next year (1875) came the Zoological Garden in Cincinnati.